Table of Contents

FOREWORD

This book has been transcribed from a series of sermons and Bible classes taught at the church of Christ in Estill Springs, Tennessee in 1998 and 1999. The Book of Revelation is probably the book that people want to know more about than any other in the Bible. People often say to me, "Let's study the Book of Revelation". I think the reason is that everybody who tries to read Revelation wonders what in the world it says. They are hoping that someone can tell them. Perhaps this book can help both students and Bible School teachers to meet this need.

There are religious groups that base their whole religious theology heavily upon the book of Revelation. There is a lot of discussion, a lot of debate and a lot of concern about this book. This study certainly will not answer all of the questions. There are some things that are deep enough in the scriptures that we all will be searching for the rest of our lives. We can ask the Lord about those when the time comes.

However, there are many things that we can understand. There are many beautiful things in the Book of Revelation that need not be neglected in our personal study, out of fear of the imagery in the Book. The objective of our study is number one, to catalog some of the things that are obvious. Secondly, study some of the things that are symbolic, but interpreted by the book itself, and thirdly to provide a top down structure for contemplation of the present day use for the things we will not be certain of for a while. It is my personal belief that the book of Revelation is a blessing from God and contains teachings that are of great present-day value to the Christian.

There is an abstract which is transcribed from a thirty minute summary sermon that takes us all the way through Revelation. It is good as an overview of the book and will give us the lay of the land before we start a detailed study. Whenever we get lost in the trees, it is always good to rise above the forest and reorient ourselves. Following that is a chapter of preliminaries that covers some basic ideas we will use throughout the study. The remainder of the book contains detailed looks at each chapter of Revelation.

As we enter this adventure of searching out the Book of Revelation, I want to begin by offering my thanks to God for his marvelous word and the gift of our intellect and ability to understand. Many thanks also goes to my daughter Renee Galloway who encouraged me to finish this and provided the illustration for the cover; to my wonderful wife Carolyn for support, editing and grammar; to Kimberly Stewart for the transcription of this material; and my preaching associate Winston Tipps, and brother in Christ David Ellenburg for their technical and scriptural editing.

All Bible quotations are taken from the New King James Version of Thomas Nelson Publishers unless otherwise noted.

INTRODUCTION

The name Revelation means to reveal or to uncover. It comes from the Greek word apocalypse. An apocalypse is a lifting of the veil. So as you would anticipate, Revelation is a book of prophecy. But this book is more than prophecy. Several of the book's chapters are not prophetic in nature. For instance, the letters to the seven churches in chapters 2 and 3 are letters that have very pointed lessons applicable to all churches today, but they were written specifically to seven very real churches. The letters deal with the spiritual condition that these churches were in at the time that this book was written. However, they also reflect upon the spiritual condition and need for healing of the church in the world today. There have been people who have attempted to take the seven churches and make them prophetic as seven different ages of the church, but there is no evidence for that in the book. The letters do not indicate that they are prophetic, and we will not deal with them as prophecy.

Two different ideas exist as to when John wrote the book of Revelation. One idea is that it was written during the time of Nero. Emperor Nero of Rome was a great persecutor of the church in the mid 60's. AD 64 and AD 67 have been proposed as the date of writing. This early writing is supported by references in Chapter 19 to the temple and to the altar. This would indicate that Jerusalem was still standing and dates the book to before AD 70 when Rome destroyed Jerusalem and the temple.

Other scholars believe a later date because some of the early church fathers of the 100s and 200s infer that the Book of Revelation was written in the 90's during the reign of Domitian. Iranaeus (AD175) suggests a date of AD 95, 96 during the reign of Domitian. Eusebius (AD260) suggests it was during the persecution of Domitian that John was banished to Patmos (Rev 1:9). Patmos is a rocky island in the Greek Archipelago southwest of Ephesus.

Domitian was a terrible persecutor of Christianity. He intensified the persecution of Christians over and above what Nero had done. Some 40,000 Christians were killed during the reign of Domitian. It has been proposed that during this reign of Domitian that John was exiled to the island of Patmos and received these visions and wrote them for the seven churches in Asia Minor.

Revelation is often compared to the Old Testament books of Daniel, Ezekiel, and Zachariah. During this study, we will be making references to some of the visions that are very similar to the visions in the Book of Revelation. This style of apocalyptic writing, where there are visions and symbols which have other meanings were very common among the Jewish writers of the centuries from 100 BC to about 200 AD, a period of about 300 years. This very popular Jewish style was adopted in the Book of Revelation. There were secular books as well that have this apocalyptic flair. A couple of the books, referred to as apocryphal books, between the Old and New Testament in Catholic Bibles are sometimes considered as apocalyptic literature.

As we study Revelation, our first attempt will be to let the Bible interpret itself rather than try to come up with some human interpretation. It is better to let the Bible tell what it means when you can. Therefore, as we study this book, we are going to be looking first to the Bible to tell us what the symbols represent.

REVELATION ABSTRACT

The Book of Revelation is a book of prophecy. It includes events for this day and time. God gave us Revelation as a book of hope. A book that would build the patience of the saints so that they could withstand the battle with the devil as he goes about the streets as a roaring lion seeking whom he may devour.

Many avoid the Book of Revelation because it is difficult to understand. It is a book that requires detailed reading, study and contemplation. There are things in the Book of Revelation that none of us will understand until God himself reveals them to us. There are things that will puzzle us until the end of time because that is the nature of prophecy. Prophecy is always better seen in hindsight and understood after it has happened.

One major difficulty with understanding the Book of Revelation is determining its chronology. Man is very interested in time. So many things in our world are measured by time. As an engineer, I make calculations where time is one of the variables, but time is not real. You may think it is real, but it is not. If I were to establish a colony on Mars, time would be totally different. There would not be 24 hours in a day and 7 days in a week. As a matter of fact, time can be very confusing. Consider traveling to the other side of the world and observing what time it is. It is a different time. It could even be a different day there than here.

There is no such thing as time. God is timeless. We simply invented time as a method of measuring the days of our lives. It really does not exist. However, we use time to arrange chronology and to organize how things fit together. One of the key challenges of the Book of Revelation is determining its timeline. This study introduces the concept that the Book of Revelation uses flashback, a technique sometimes seen in movies today. In a flashback, the story will be taken back to an earlier period of time and brought forward. This study in the Book of Revelation will identify those flashbacks and use them effectively in the interpretation of the book.

There are many interpretive methods that have been used to explain the Book of Revelation. One of them insists that the Book of Revelation only deals with the fall of the Roman Empire and the destruction of Jerusalem and was written for first century Christians about first century events. They draw that conclusion from the very first verse of the Book of Revelation where it says that these things shall shortly take place, and also from the third verse where it says that the time is near. There are others who refuse that approach and reference verse 19 of chapter 1 where it says, "Write the things which you have seen, and the things which are, and the things which will take place after this." The conclusion is that there is a history of the whole world here. Then they struggle to build a time line that marks such things as World War I and World War II and the Holocaust. Many attempt to tie things in the Book of Revelation to physical worldly events that have occurred in our history.

The time line used for reference in this book is not one I have learned from someone else. It is one that has been deduced from personal study. So take it for what it is worth. Revelation is authored by God, but this interpretation is by this fallible author. So if after you have evaluated the approach, you don't think it has merit, just throw the book away. My goal is to offer the approach to you as a method of looking at what God is telling us about his eternal plan for the world and most importantly, that the Kingdom of Heaven will not be shaken and God is ultimately victorious.

Figure 1 is a graphical representation of the proposed timeline for Revelation. The flashbacks are shown in columns with time proceeding from the top of the chart to the bottom. References to the Revelation chapters will tie together the timeline as we study the details through the book.

A Timeline of the Revelation Visions

1 Introduction of Christ					T
2-3 Letters to the Churches					I
4 The Throne Room					M
5-Sealed Book/Lamb					E
6 *Heaven* 1st Seal – White Horse/ Bow/ Crown/ Conqueror 2nd Seal Red Horse/ take peace/ sword/ kill 3rd Seal – Black Horse/ Scales 4th Seal – Pale Horse Death/ Hades 5th Seal – Saints – 6:10 How Long How Long – rest a little longer 6th Seal – Moon to blood		12 *Earth* Woman Fiery Red Dragon War in Heaven Devil cast to Earth War on Earth – Devils war on the woman and her offspring 13 Beast of Sea – Pride of Life Beast of Earth – Lust of Eyes Babylon – Lust of Flesh			
7 144,000 and Great Multitude – out of tribulation washed robes 7:14	11 Two witnesses	14 144,000 vs 6 – Gospel to preach to all who dwell on the earth vs 9 – warning against the devil Harvest		20 Flashback Devil bound for 1000 years	
8 7th Seal –Trumpets of Judgment Trumpets 1-4 9 Trumpets 5-6 10 little book	Trumpet 7 The End	15 Seven bowls of Judgment prepared 16 Bowls 1-7 The End	17/18 Flashback What about the destruction of Babylon? 19 Christ's Coming and the Judgment – The End	Satan judged The End	
21-22 New Heaven and New Earth					

The Revelation Chronology

This abstract of the Revelation study will take you completely through the book in the next few pages. So grab hold and hang on, because it is going to be fast. These highlights are intended to interest you enough that you will want to complete the study detailed in the remainder of this book; and having studied will have the words "Hallelujah Anyway" well up in your heart. That is really the theme of Revelation when we realize that God is in control and will be victorious. We will learn that the devil and his angels and those with his mark will be thrown into the lake of fire and brimstone.

In Chapter 1 of Revelation we are introduced to the Lord Jesus Christ. Every book in the Bible is about Jesus, but this book in particular is authored by Jesus with His secretary, John. Jesus told John, "What you see, write in a book and send it to the seven churches which are in Asia." Chapter 1 contains a beautiful picture of Jesus which is the only photograph we have of Him in the Bible. You see artists' pictures of Jesus with His long hair and long beard and facial features that do not look Jewish and wonder who imagined that. Nonetheless, the Bible does tell us what Jesus looks like in Chapter 1. This chapter also describes the purpose and scope of Revelation.

Chapters 2 and 3 reveal Jesus' letters to the seven churches of Asia Minor. These letters are instructions that illustrate that even in the first century, churches were dealing with problems much like we have today. The churches had good qualities and bad qualities. These two chapters show how those seven churches were instructed directly from the words of Jesus Christ and how they could overcome those things that were oppressing them. These churches serve as good and bad examples for the church of today.

In chapter 4, John begins in exile on the Isle of Patmos and was lifted up into Heaven and shown a great vision. This vision begins in the beautiful throne room of God, where John introduces the four living creatures that fly around the throne and the twenty-four elders who sit around the throne. He describes the great sea of crystal that is in front of the throne. It is an inspiring picture of God on His throne in the throne room.

In Chapter 5, John sees a book that is sealed with seven seals. We will discuss a great deal about numerology, (that is, the use of numbers) in the Book of Revelation, but suffice it for now that numbers are not just for counting. Numbers represent ideas and concepts to the Jewish mind. The number seven represents completeness. Seven of anything is complete; and the fact that there were seven seals on this book indicates that it is a complete revelation that is completely sealed. There was nothing you could see. It was like those Christmas presents which you double wrap. You can rub your hand across them but you cannot see through two layers of paper. You cannot see what is underneath. Maybe it was wrapped in a big box so you cannot feel what it is and stuffed with tissue paper so that it does not even rattle. You cannot tell what is inside. That is the way this book was. It was sealed with seven seals. John began to cry because no one was worthy to open that book and he wanted to know so badly what was inside. Then, the lamb appeared; the Lamb of God; the Lord Jesus Christ. The Lord Jesus Christ was worthy to open that book and to reveal the things to John that were, that are and that are going to be.

This first vision recorded in Chapters 5 thru 11, as the seals are opened, is a vision of the history of the world from a spiritual viewpoint. It is intended to emphasize that there is, and since creation has been, a battle between the forces of good and evil. God has allowed this battle to rage to show the foolishness of evil and to show that ultimately good overcomes evil.

In the Book of Job, when the devil came from walking to and fro upon the Earth; he came into the presence of God and God asked,

> "Have you considered My servant Job, that there is none like him on the earth, a blameless and upright man, one who fears God and shuns evil?"

The devil said,

> "Does Job fear God for nothing? Have You not made a hedge around him, around his household, and around all that he has on every side? You have blessed the work of his hands, and his possessions have increased in the land. But now, stretch out Your hand and touch all that he has, and he will surely curse You to Your face!"

The devil was able to walk into the presence of God. That is an interesting point. The devil was one of the angels of God. In fact, if you believe Ezekiel 28 refers to the devil, you would see that this devil was more beautiful than any of the angels and he became so prideful over his own beauty that he wanted to be God. That is the product he is still selling on the Earth. He would like each one of you to think that you can be God and that you do not need your Heavenly Father. He wants you to believe that you can handle it all by yourself. That is one of his poisonous lies that he tries to sell. That is the lie that he sold that drove him from heaven and Adam and Eve out of Eden.

The first seal on the scroll is removed and out rides a white horse. On the white horse is a rider who carries a bow and has a crown on his head and is called a conqueror. Later on in the Book of Revelation, there is another vision where a man is seen on a white horse, and the Revelator tells us that it is the Lord Jesus Christ. So, when this first seal is opened, what we see coming forth is Jesus, Jesus on a white horse. The white horse being ridden by Jesus, the crowned King, represents purity and goodness.

The second seal is opened and out comes a red horse. The rider on the red horse is carrying a sword and he is to take the peace from the Earth and he is to kill. The color red in the Book of Revelation often refers to the devil and those beasts that worship the devil. What is introduced when the first seal is opened is good; Jesus manifesting the goodness of God. The second seal is opened and manifests evil; the devil and all the wickedness he brings. They are on horses and they have implements of war and there is going to be a great battle between good and evil. In Ephesians 6:17, Paul describes the Christian armor. He recorded that we fight in a battle that is not an earthly or worldly battle. We fight in a battle that is against principalities and powers and evil forces in heavenly places. So, there is a heavenly battle that is to take place, a battle between good and evil.

When the third seal is opened a rider on a black horse emerges. The rider on the black horse has a set of scales in his hand. Those scales represent judgment. There is going to be a judgment between good and evil. The battle is going to decide the victor to be either good or evil. We have to make choices everyday in our lives between good and evil. Evil destroys us. The wages of sin is death, but the free gift of God is eternal life through Christ Jesus, our Lord. There is a judgment being made in our own lives between what is good and what is evil.

Out of the fourth seal comes a rider on a pale horse. A pale horse whose rider is described as death, and Hades follows him. One of the things that happened in the battle between the devil and Jesus Christ was that Jesus died. The Psalmist has said that Jesus' soul could not be kept in Hades, the place of the dead. Jesus said he would be there three days and three nights and then he would be raised from the dead. In Genesis 3:15, God gives us an insight into what is going to happen. God told Satan,

> *"And I will put enmity between you and the woman, and between your seed and her Seed; He shall bruise your head, and you shall bruise His heel."*

The message is that the offspring of Eve, namely Jesus, is going to bruise the head of Satan. He is going to deliver a blow to the head, a death blow to Satan, the serpent. However, in that process, his heel is going to be bruised. Death will come to Jesus in the battle between good and evil. The devil causes the Lord Jesus Christ to be crucified and to die a cruel death on the cross. As a result however, Satan lost the battle because he caused an innocent man to be crucified. He crucified a man who had no sin. So with the fourth seal comes the message of the death that is going to come to the Savior.

The fifth seal is opened in Revelation 6:10 and reveals saints who are crying out;

> *"How long, O Lord, holy and true, until You judge and avenge our blood on those who dwell on the earth?"*

In Hebrews Chapter 11, the Hebrew writer describes all of the faithful people who had lived in the world before the time of Christ and how they cried out to understand the prophecies that were within them. He said that they died all kind of terrible deaths, yet not seeing the thing that they had their faith and trust in. They were crying how long do we have to put up with this evil? How long do we have to bear with this wickedness? The message came back to them and said,

> *"Rest a little while longer."*

As the sixth seal was opened, there were earthquakes; great tremors and catastrophes on the earth. Then the moon turned to blood. Peter tells us what that means in Acts chapter 2. He described the events that the people had seen at the death of the Lord Jesus Christ. Peter quoted an Old Testament prophet and talked about how the moon had turned to blood and that they had seen it. The message is clear here that the sixth seal is talking about the death, the burial and the resurrection of the Lord Jesus Christ. Death and Hades on the pale horse comes and takes its toll, but Jesus is resurrected from the dead. In Chapter 7, in the midst of the sixth seal, the moon has turned to blood.

Then there are 144,000 out of the nation of Israel who are sealed that become the servants of righteousness. There are 12,000 from the tribe of Reuben; 12,000 from the tribe of Levi; 12,000 from the tribe of Judah and so on, all down through all twelve of the sons of Jacob, making a total of 144,000 servants of righteousness. The next verse explains that there would also be a great multitude of all nations. Brethren, if I had to point my finger somewhere, and say that is where we are right now, I would put my finger right here in Chapter 7. That is where the sealing of the saints is going on. That is where the great gospel is being preached to the whole world. That is where we are right now. We are in Chapter 7 and the gospel is being preached. Out of that great tribulation come those who have their robes washed in the blood of the lamb and who wear white robes. These are those who belong to the Kingdom that comes in contact with the blood of the Lord Jesus Christ.

In Chapter 8, the seventh seal is opened and out comes seven trumpets. Trumpets are used to announce the coming of something. As Paul wrote to the Thessalonians, he said that the Lord would come with His mighty angels taking vengeance on those that know not God and obey not the Gospel and He would come with the sound of a trumpet. Here are the trumpets, the trumpets of Judgment. Trumpets one through four are sounded in Chapter 8. Trumpets five and six are sounded in Chapter 9, and finally trumpet number seven is sounded in Chapter 11. These trumpets announce the end of the world, the judgment of God.

We see encapsulated here, the fact that the forces of good and the forces of evil are going to be doing a battle and judgment is made. That Judgment is through the death of Jesus Christ, His burial, and after that His resurrection. There is to be a sowing of the seed into the entire world so that they can come to repentance; so that they can wear white robes and then judgment will come. The judgment will come at the sound of trumpets with terrible things happening to this earth and to the heavens. Peter said that this earth and the heavens will pass away with a fervent heat.

The picture painted of the judgment of God and the end of the world is in Revelation chapter 11. When you get halfway through the book of Revelation, you are finished with the history of the world. In the map of the chronology previously shown, we return to the top of the second column and pick up with Chapter 12 where we are flashed back and the vision begins over again. This time, the vision is telling the history of the world from an earthly or physical perspective. The left column of the chronology is a heavenly perspective and the second column is an earthy perspective of the same history of the world.

What was it like to be on earth when this great battle of good and evil was going on? John says it was like a woman who was pregnant with child. That woman is the nation of Israel. She was God's chosen nation for almost 4,000 years until the fullness of time. Then the child, the promised child,

Jesus, would come and be the Savior. But there was a great red dragon that came down and stood and waited for the child to be born. He troubled Israel awaiting the birth of the child. Then he battled Jesus when He was born, especially as recorded in Matthew 4. The devil could not wait to get his hands on Jesus. He could not wait to tempt the Son of God. He tried every way he could to cause the Son of God to fail. He tried to make him fear death. He brought great grief upon Him. He made Jesus face a terrible, terrible death. The devil unleashed upon Christ demons that possessed people. The devil was allowed great authority and power upon the earth. The Devil is referred to as the Prince of this earth. He offered Jesus everything in the whole world. It was his to give. It belonged to him. All Satan had to do was to get Jesus to turn to him and he would have won the heavenly battle. But Jesus would not turn to Satan.

While that fiery red dragon was doing battle against the woman, the Revelator reports that there was war in Heaven. Michael and his angels waged that war with Satan and his angels. The moon turning to blood, the great earthquakes on the Earth, the great struggle and darkness that went on in the world at the death of Jesus Christ are all artifacts of a tremendous war that was being waged between the Devil and God, and God's angels and the Devil's angels. Jesus said that He saw Satan fall from Heaven like lightning. After that, Satan was bound deprived of the powers he had over the earth. The blood of Jesus and the word of His testimony left Satan powerless over anyone who resisted him. After Satan crucified Jesus, an innocent man, His death became a sacrifice that destroyed the dominion of Satan on the earth. He was no longer able to possess men as he did during the time of Christ.

Satan lost the war, the war whose ultimate victory was Jesus Christ resurrected from Hades. Then, because Satan had lost the war, the devil did battle against the woman. Still filled with pride, he tried to destroy everything that belonged to God. He tried to destroy Israel. He used the Roman Empire and crushed the nation of Israel. The beautiful city of Jerusalem and the temple were destroyed. The Jewish people lost their home and no more would be called upon as a great nation. Revelation Chapter 12 reveals that the devil poured out a great flood against Israel and that the Earth swallowed it up. The devil grew angrier and persecuted the offspring of the woman. The offspring of Israel is you and me. It is spiritual Israel, the Kingdom of Christ, the church.

The devil is like a roaring lion walking to and fro upon the earth seeking whom he may devour. He is angry. He is angry because he is defeated. He is angry because he is bound and powerless against those who believe in Jesus. He is angry because he knows what waits on him, and he wants to take as many of us with him as he can. His spite and his hatred want to draw us away from the God who loves us and protects us. He is bound; he is helpless against those who love Christ; but he can still have his way with those outside Christ and those who fail to endure.

Then, beginning in Chapter 13, we are warned of the tools of the devil that he uses as he wages war against you and me. The first tool is the beast that came from the sea. The beast that came from the sea is described in very graphic terms. In the Bible, the sea is usually interpreted as a multitude, a great number of people. This beast, this monster, came up out of the multitude of people. Those able to identify this beast better than anybody else is our teenagers. They see this beast every day. He rises up out of the high school and preaches that everybody is doing it. It is a beast that is a tool of the devil. It is the beast of the pride of life. It is the beast that rises up and says I want you to be like me. I want you to dress like the masses. I want you to act like the multitudes. I want you to follow the latest fads. I want you to try all of the things that there are on this Earth. You are god. You are in control of your destiny and in control of your life. This beast begs for you to worship the devil.

Then there is a second beast that rises up out of the earth. This beast causes you to worship the first beast (the pride of life) by offering you the things of the earth (the lust of the eyes). I would like to have that new car. What I wouldn't give for it. How I would like to have that big fancy house. Could I cheat on my income tax and get that? This beast is the Devil's tool known as the lust of the eyes. The lust of what I can see drives me to want to be someone that is full of pride, making me want to worship the first beast.

The third beast is called Babylon, and is depicted as a city full of adultery and harlots. It is a city full of wickedness and pleasures of the flesh. It is the city that typifies the lust of the flesh. The devil uses these three tools to seduce us and to draw us away from God. He lies and tells us that it will make us feel good. He tells us it is enjoyable. It is the devil telling you a lie. These are the tools of the devil that have come to destroy mankind upon the Earth. These tools of the devil John described in 1 John 2:15, where he says that the things that are of the world and not of God are the lust of the flesh, the lust of the eyes and the pride of life. These tools of the Devil are the beasts that the Revelator describes.

Chapter 14 leaves the beasts and turns our attention to the angels that come forth and preach an everlasting gospel. Chapter 14 reminds us that they are going to draw 144,000 out of the nation of Israel and a great multitude out of all of the nations of the Earth. Does that sound like anything you have read before? Yes, we just finished talking about that in Chapter 7. You will notice that if you look at the flashback chronology, that Chapter 7 is right across from Chapter 14. They are both writing about the same events paralleling the heavenly vision with the earthly vision.

We are warned not to follow the devil. The gospel is going to be preached to all of the people on the Earth. We receive warning about following after the devil and then there will be a harvest. The angels will have sickles, blades on the end of a stick, which are used to harvest wheat. The angels will harvest the Earth. Jesus will come forth with a sickle and also harvest the Earth. The fields are white unto harvest, Jesus said. He instructed us to,

> *"Go into all the world and preach the gospel to every creature. He who believes and is baptized will be saved; but he who does not believe will be condemned."*

Put your finger right there in the middle of Chapter 14. That is where we are now in the history of the world.

In Chapter 15, angels bring seven bowls that are referred to as seven bowls of judgment. They are prepared in Chapter 15 and in Chapter 16 they are poured out upon the Earth. They bring the destruction of the earth and the destruction of the heavens. The sea is destroyed and all of the sea animals are destroyed. All of the wild life is destroyed, as all of the trees and plants and then comes the end. We saw the end of the world and God's judgment in Chapter 11. The end is seen again in Chapter 16 in this flashback vision with an earthly perspective.

In Chapter 17, it is as though John asked the question; I saw the first two beasts die, but what about Babylon? So, we have another flashback. In Chapter 17 and 18, a flashback takes us back in time and shows the destruction of Babylon and all of the lustful things that exist upon the earth.

In Chapter 19 we see the judgment of God again as John describes Christ's coming. He comes on a white horse for the judgment in a second throne room scene. We get a third look at the end of the world in Chapter 19 which is a parallel with Chapter 16 and Chapter 11.

Then John would want to know what would become of the devil. Chapter 20 flashes us back again into the past. It flashes back in time to when the Devil fell from Heaven. Recall the Great War with Michael, back in Chapter 12, where the devil was thrown from Heaven. Chapter 20 reveals that he was placed in a bottomless pit and chained. His powers were taken away. The Saints begin a 1,000 year reign. Some people teach that this millennium starts when Jesus comes again to establish a kingdom on this Earth. If Jesus was going to do that, He would have done it the first time. The Bible teaches that Jesus is sitting at the right hand of the throne of God and that He is King of Kings and Lord of Lords. It teaches that His kingdom exists upon this earth this very day. It is not an earthly kingdom. It is not a physical nation that is going to rise up. It is where we live now and the devil is bound. The Devil is walking to and fro, trying to find somebody he can devour because he can no longer possess you. He has no power over you. The Bible teaches that if we resist the devil, he will flee from us. The devil's power has been removed. He is chained for 1,000 years, and Christians have the opportunity to plant the earth for the harvest. For 1,000 years, we have the opportunity to preach the everlasting gospel. Of course the 1,000 years is not literal. With God, 1,000 years is as a day and a day as 1,000 years.

We have the opportunity to tell the world that God wins. You can know the end of the story before the end gets there. God wins. I get frustrated with football games because I start pulling for a team and they lose. Sometimes, I think I am bad luck. So, I decided that I just won't pull for any teams. Wouldn't it be a treat if you knew who was going to win before you went to the game? You would know what side of the field to sit on.

In this world, we know who is going to win. God is the victor and the devil is already bound. He can have no power over you except the power you give to him. The Book of Revelation makes us aware of that, for he is bound for this 1,000 year Christian era. In Chapter 20 Satan is judged. God judges him and throws him into outer darkness where there is weeping and gnashing of teeth. Satan and his angels are sent to a lake that burns with fire and brimstone; a lake that is removed from the presence of God forever. The judgment day then brings all those wicked ones who have followed after the devil and places them with the devil where they belong. We see the end of the world recorded once more in Chapter 20.

In Chapter 21 and 22, the Revelator is shown what is next. The Earth is melted with a fervent heat. The heavens are burned up. Satan is cast into a lake of fire with his angels and with all of those who bear his mark on their forehead. Then, from heaven comes New Jerusalem. A beautiful city adorned for all of the Saints, a city foursquare; a city in which there is no weeping and no crying and no sorrow; a city in which the light is God; a city in which the river of life flows through the midst of it and the trees of life grow and bear their fruits in all seasons. Those who live there shall never die. Heaven is a wonderful sight.

God has shown us the whole script. God has shown us where we are. Here is the patience of the saints. The patience of the Saints is in knowing that God is in control and knowing that God is victorious. "Hallelujah Anyway!"

PRELIMINARIES

The Blessing of Reading Revelation

John begins this book with a blessing. Revelation is written to people who are being persecuted, tortured and oppressed for their Christianity. His message is a message of hope. The message is validated by the presence of angels and contains the words of Jesus Christ. Assurance is given that the suffering is but for a little while. Blessed is the one who reads and hears the words of this prophecy. This book is written to make you happy. The word, blessed, means happy. The purpose of this book is to bring joy to those who read it; for them to understand that God's plan is in force even though they are suffering. That ultimately God is victorious and that God's will is being done. Sometimes, that is a little hard for us when we are struggling, but we will be blessed by seeing God's plan revealed in Revelation.

The seven blessings (Beatitudes) of Revelation are:

- Revelation 1:3 *"Blessed is he who reads and those who hear the words of this prophecy and keep those things, which are written in it for the time is near;"*
- Revelation 14:13 *"Blessed are the dead that die in the Lord;"*
- Revelation 16:15 *"Behold, I am coming as a thief, blessed is he who watches;"*
- Revelation 19:9. *"He said to me write blessed are those who are called to the marriage supper of the lamb."*
- Revelation 20:6. *"Blessed and holy is he who is a part in the first resurrection over such the second death has no power,"*
- Revelation 22:7 *"Behold, I come quickly, blessed is he who keeps the words of the prophecy of this book;"*
- Revelation 22:14. *"Blessed are they who do His commandments that they might have the right to the tree of life and may enter through the gates into the city;"*

Revelation is addressed to the seven churches, which are in Asia. In chapter 1, verse eleven, Jesus addresses the churches by name. They are Ephesus, Smyrna, Pergamos, Thyatira, Sardis, Philadelphia and Laodicea. Asia Minor is east of Greece and includes modern day Turkey. To the south, in the Mediterranean Sea, is an island named Patmos, where John was exiled and then wrote Revelation.

John has been shown things which must shortly take place and the time is near. John hasn't just been shown things that are in the distant future, but things that first century Christians would want to know and draw hope from. Some have suggested this to mean events of the end time were going to take place very soon; but looking back from 2,000 years later it is obvious that is not the case. In verse nineteen, John is instructed to write the things which he has seen, and the things which are, and the things which will take place after this. Many interpret the Book of Revelation as all about the future. However, John is told to write about the past, the present and the future. The directive of the book is to reveal the planning of God in the past, the present and the future. The Book of Revelation is a panorama. It is seeing the history roll before you that God has prepared from the foundation of the world until the end of time. The result is that we gain insight into why God did all this and what part we play in his plan. We gain insight into why the struggle is now and how God will be ultimately victorious. We are blessed by knowing. We can endure the struggle because we know the whole story.

Revelation Interpretations

Revelation is apocalyptic. It is imagery. It is full of things like falling stars, dragons, creatures with ten heads and ten crowns, candlesticks and lights on the candlesticks. How do we understand what it all means? There have been numerous approaches to the interpretation of the Book of Revelation. Four of them are predominant.

One is referred to as the Spiritual interpretation. It is a philosophical interpretation in which the images do not stand for real things. The images stand for ideas and philosophies. It pictures good and evil and the battle between good and evil.

Another is called the Preterist view. It advocates that every symbol is about things that shortly come to pass. Preterists believe everything in the Book of Revelation is about the fall of the Roman Empire, occurred in the first few centuries, and all of the prophecies are fulfilled. They believe that God was victorious over Rome, established his kingdom, and the Book of Revelation ended.

A third approach, the Historical interpretation takes each symbol as something that has happened in history. The historical approach finds symbols in Revelation to be people and battles, world wars and even Hitler. They label political characters as the antichrist even though an antichrist is not mentioned in the Book of Revelation.

The Futurist interpretation represents a fourth approach to the Book of Revelation. This interpretation originated in the nineteenth century and builds great sweeping descriptions of the time when Christ is going to come again. They apply the prophecies and visions to the end time. Differing views have gained names such as pre-millennial, post millennial, a-millennial, all of these dealing with 1,000 years (millennium) in Revelation Chapter 20.

We are not going to use any of these four major interpretive views. We are going to take a fifth view. I stand in jeopardy with this view because it is my view. It is a result of the studies that I have done in the Book of Revelation that do not fit any of the previous patterns. It is the reason for this book about Revelation.

The major emphasis of this interpretation is to put Jesus in it. Jesus is in the first chapter. Jesus is in the last chapter and Jesus appears many times in the book of Revelation such that we gain great insight about Him. We find Him as a Lamb. We find Him riding a white horse and conquering. We find Him as King of Kings and Lord of Lords. We find Him worthy. In Verse five, it says the book is from Jesus Christ, the faithful witness, the first born from the dead and the ruler over the kings of the earth. That was written in the first century and says that Jesus is the ruler of all of the kings of the earth. Some believe that Christ has to come back and conquer all of the kings but John reveals in Jesus' words that He is already the ruler of all kings. Revelation reveals to me that God is in charge of everything. God is in control.

A friend at work during the last presidential election said to me "I know that God is in charge of the outcome of this election. What I can't figure out is whether God is going to let us elect the one that will reward us or the one that will punish us." Even the Old Testament prophets wondered why the Lord was blessing a heathen nation. God responded that it was because the heathen nation was going to reap judgment on His people because of their unfaithfulness. God is in charge. He is in charge of the good rulers and the bad rulers. When I see bad rulers it does not mean that God is not in charge.

This interpretation will set the pattern from the beginning. The book is about Jesus the conqueror. That Jesus is sitting at the right hand of the throne of God. That Jesus is our advocate. That Jesus is speaking for us. That even those who die persecuted for their Christianity, will be gathered around the throne of God in that eternal kingdom. This is the blessing, the good news. Perhaps the Book of Revelation should be called "Hallelujah Anyway." It doesn't matter what is happening around me, "Hallelujah Anyway". God is in charge. God is in control. To God belongs the victory.

Revelation Numerology

As you read Revelation, you will soon realize that even the numbers seem to be symbolic. We have difficulty with this concept because our culture is so different. In Old and New Testament times, people did count with numbers. They counted money. They counted all sorts of things. They had mathematics, things like the Pythagorean Theorem and a wealth of mathematical knowledge that we still use today. The number systems that were developed in that time, we still use today; but their interest in numbers was not just for counting. When we think about numbers, we think about counting. When we read that the Lord is going to reign for 1,000 years, we think of a literal counting 1,000 years. To understand Revelation we need to appreciate how the Jewish mind considered numbers. For example, in the Book of Deuteronomy, we read, "The Lord our God, the Lord is one!" Paul wrote in the Book of Ephesians that there is one Lord, one faith, one baptism, one God and Father of us all. Obviously, the number one in these passages does not refer to a single thing. The Lord our God, He is one God. He is God the Father, God the Son and God the Holy Spirit. There are three of them. How can we understand that? We have to stop counting. The number one was for more than counting. It had a symbolic meaning. The number one expressed the idea of unity. When the scriptures teach that in marriage the husband and wife become one, it is not talking about merging at the hips and being Siamese. It is describing the unity of having one purpose and one mind.

The Jews used many numbers in a symbolic way. Consider the number two. To the Jew, two were stronger than one. Strength comes from having a group of people band together. They lived together for security and strength. So the number two came to represent strength. When the Book of Revelation speaks about two witnesses, somebody will ask who they were. One would say that maybe it was Moses and Elijah. Some will argue that it was the Old Testament and New Testament. We have fallen into the counting trap. The counting trap is from our culture. In the Jewish culture two witnesses were sufficient. That was enough. That was a strong witness. If two people witness the same thing, then the witness becomes strong and powerful.

The number three in the Jewish mind meant spiritual completeness. The idea of three was a family number representing mother, father, and child. It was God the Father, God the Son, and God the Holy Spirit. It was a number of perfection.

The number four referred to the world. There are four cardinal directions; north, south, east and west. When a Jew thought about God's physical creation, this number four represented the natural world. Thus, we read of four horsemen and four living creatures.

Five represented their major counting number. Five and its multiples represent human completeness. Five fingers on one hand and I am complete. Five fingers on the other hand and I am complete again. Five and ten are numbers that represent all of it. If I give you four, I have not given you all. But, if I give you five, I have given you everything. When you see a dragon that had ten heads, you know that John probably is not talking about ten successive kings that you must find. Ten conveys the idea of human completeness. That is all of them. From the beginning to the end of that kingdom would be ten.

Six is a sinister number. Seven is a perfect number made from four plus three so that included everything that is God and everything that is Man. It represents perfection. If you miss perfection or completeness by one you have the number six. Now, combine this number with how the Hebrews did superlatives.   Their language had no good, better, or best. Hebrews would repeat the word to indicate a superlative. For example good, good, good for better; and good, good, good for best. If they were describing a pretty girl they might say pretty if she was pretty. They would say pretty, pretty if she was very beautiful; and if she was just gorgeous she was pretty, pretty, pretty. That is why the Bible describes God as Holy, Holy, Holy, Lord God Almighty. That is as holy as you can get. That is the superlative. When a sinister number like six becomes six, six, six it is as evil as you can get. Six, six, six has missed the mark completely.   The concept is evil, evil, evil.

The number seven is the number of perfection. If you divide seven in half, you get three and a half. Three and a half is incomplete or imperfect. When you read of a time, times, and a half time in Revelation, remember this Jewish number concept. The number seven is very predominant in the Book of Revelation. In the first chapter, there are seven churches, seven spirits, and seven candlesticks. There are thirty-two verses with over fifty references in Revelation to the number seven. Sometimes, the number seven is not mentioned, but there will still be seven references to things. In Chapter one, we mentioned the reference to "Blessed is he who reads and those who hear the words of this prophecy." There are seven of these blessings in the Book of Revelation as we have already seen.

The number twelve is a powerful number because it is four times three. Spiritual completeness multiplied by physical completeness is the number that symbolizes organized religion (God and man's relationship). Have you ever wondered why there were twelve tribes or twelve apostles? The picking of twelve is very symbolic. It was symbolic to the Hebrew mind because they did not just use numbers to count. They used numbers as concepts. As we read through the Book of Revelation, understand that we will have to step out of our counting culture to understand what we read.

Chronological Flashback

As we study the Book of Revelation we need first to get an overview of the book, before we get buried in a lot of the details. We have already mentioned the idea of chronological flashback. The first eleven chapters represent the complete history of the world. Chapter 1 is an introduction that tells the purpose of the book, who wrote the book and why it was written. Chapters 2 and 3 are a pair that provides the letters to the seven churches. In these two chapters, Jesus, the great physician diagnoses the health of each local congregation and prescribes remedies for their sicknesses. In Chapter 4, John was in the Spirit on the Lord's Day and was called up into Heaven. Chapter 4 begins the second vision. The first vision is in Chapter 1. Chapter 4 begins the vision from Heaven, which continues all of the way through to Chapter 11. The visions can be broken down into groups of seven. Remember that seven is not a counting number but conveys the idea of completeness. The first vision has seven candlesticks for seven churches. The second vision has seven seals and out of the seventh seal comes seven trumpets. The seven trumpets are the judgment of God. In chapter 11, God's temple is open in Heaven, representing the end of this physical world.

From Chapter 12 through 20, there is a third vision. It begins with the description of a woman who is about to bear a child and a great dragon who is there to consume the child as soon as it is born. Remember, when you study the Book of Revelation you need to put Jesus in it. The whole Bible is about Jesus. And so, we read about a woman with child about to give birth and a dragon, which the Book of Revelation says is Satan, the devil. The devil is seeking to consume that child. So the child is Jesus, and the woman is Israel. In the Book of Galatians God speaks of the fullness of time when Christ died for the ungodly. The fullness of time means God's plan. God has a timetable for the coming of Jesus. Jesus was promised in Genesis Chapter 3 to be the seed of woman. In Genesis Chapter 12, we read that Abraham is going to have a great nation and out of that nation all nations are going to be blessed. Paul makes the argument in the New Testament that the seed promise of Jesus was not given directly to Abraham, but it was given to his seed, and that through his seed all nations would be blessed. It was the prophecy that the Savior would be a child of Abraham, a child of the nation of Israel. The devil, when he could not destroy Jesus, attacked the woman and a great struggle followed. In chapter 12 we read about a war in Heaven. This war in Heaven is alluded to in the Book of Jude. Michael, the Archangel, was the commander of the army of God and Satan and his angels fought against them. Jesus said, I know Michael was victorious in that battle because I saw that serpent, Satan, fall from Heaven as lightning.

Chapter 12 thru 16 is parallel to chapter 4 through 11 and recites the history again from an earthly perspective. Again, there are seven bowls that bring the destruction of the world and the seventh bowl has seven woes. In chapter 16 earth is destroyed and we come to the end of the world being described a second time.

Then, like in a novel, the author goes back and summarizes what happened to each of the individual characters. Sometimes in a movie you will see this done The movie will note that this was inspired by a real story and then trace you through what happened to all of the people who were the main characters in the story. John does the same thing. Starting in chapter 17, he tells us what happens in the judgment of the great harlot. In chapter 18 we see the judgment of those who would oppose God. Chapter 19 provides that victorious marriage supper of the lamb and the victory of all of those who had been rescued from the oppression and destruction of the world.

Chapter 20 parallels with chapter 17 and tells us what becomes of the devil. We have seen the end of the servants of the devil on the earth who were tempting and trying to destroy man. The Devil who is Satan or Lucifer finds his Waterloo in this chapter. Then, Chapters 21 and 22 rehearse our ultimate destiny in the new Heaven and new Earth for the old heaven and earth have passed away.

REVELATION - CHAPTER 1

Chapter 1 of Revelation introduces the purpose and scope that John through the Holy Spirit from Jesus Christ put into this book. In Verse 1, John is told that these things must shortly take place. In Verse 3, he continues with "for the time is near." Obviously, there are things in the book that were very timely when they were written. Then, in Verse 19, John is told, "Write the things which you have seen, and the things which are, and the things which will take place after this." John is instructed to record the things that are in the past, the things which are in the present, and the things that are to come to pass in the future. The Book of Revelation is revealing history from creation until judgment.

John is introduced as the writer of the book in verse 1. John is the writer, but the author is Jesus. Jesus appears to John while he is exiled on the island of Patmos and instructs him to be His secretary and write down the things that are going to be revealed, the things that he sees and the subsequent visions. John recites,

> *"And He sent and signified it by His angel to His servant John, who bore witness to the word of God, and to the testimony of Jesus Christ, to all things that he saw."*

In Verse 4, he reintroduces himself as "

> *John, to the seven churches which are in Asia."*

In Verse 9, John introduces himself for the third time as;

> *"I, John, both your brother and companion in the tribulation and kingdom and patience of Jesus Christ."*

Between the first and second introduction is the blessing of reading the book. Between the second and third introduction he describes Jesus as the faithful witness. He has introduced himself three times with an interlude between each. John is showing these interludes as an organizational framework for the book in the very first chapter.

Verse 10 locates John on the isle of Patmos in the Spirit on the Lord's Day when he hears behind him a loud voice as a trumpet and began his visions. In verses 10 through 16 John reveals the vision of Jesus, a veritable portrait of the Messiah in heaven. How we like the early disciples, long to see Jesus. In John 12:21 we read;

> *"Then they came to Philip, who was from Bethsaida of Galilee, and asked him, saying, 'Sir, we wish to see Jesus.'"*

In Hebrews 2:9, the scripture pictures Jesus as a man;

"But we see Jesus, who was made a little lower than the angels, for the suffering of death crowned with glory and honor, that He, by the grace of God, might taste death for everyone."

Jesus is pictured as the Son of Man eighty times in the Gospels. Stephen saw Jesus in heaven in Acts 7:56 as the son of man and said;

"Look! I see the heavens opened and the Son of Man standing at the right hand of God!"

John's vision was similar when he said in Revelation 1:13;

"...and in the midst of the seven lampstands One like the Son of Man, clothed with a garment down to the feet and girded about the chest with a golden band."

Also in Revelation 14:14;

"Then I looked, and behold, a white cloud, and on the cloud sat One like the Son of Man, having on His head a golden crown, and in His hand a sharp sickle

John's word picture of Jesus is painted in the first chapter in verses 13 thru 16

"and in the midst of the seven lampstands One like the Son of Man, clothed with a garment down to the feet and girded about the chest with a golden band. His head and hair were white like wool, as white as snow, and His eyes like a flame of fire; His feet were like fine brass, as if refined in a furnace, and His voice as the sound of many waters; He had in His right hand seven stars, out of His mouth went a sharp two-edged sword, and His countenance was like the sun shining in its strength."

These seven characteristics of Jesus become the introductions of Jesus when he writes to the seven churches in chapters 2 and 3. These seven characteristics of Jesus repeated in the letters to the seven churches reinforces the parallel and repetitive nature of the telling that occurs in the Book of Revelation.

To the Church at Ephesus:

2:1 "These things says He who holds the seven stars in His right hand, who walks in the midst of the seven golden lampstands:"

To the Church at Smyrna:

2:8 "These things says the First and the Last, who was dead, and came to life:"

To the Church at Pergamos:

2:12 "These things says He who has the sharp two-edged sword:"

To the Church at Thyatira:

> *2:18 "These things says the Son of God, who has eyes like a flame of fire, and His feet like fine brass:"*

To the Church at Sardis:

> *3:1 "These things says He who has the seven Spirits of God and the seven stars:"*

To the Church at Philadelphia:

> *3:7 "These things says He who is holy, He who is true, He who has the key of David, He who opens and no one shuts, and shuts and no one opens:"*

To the Church at Laodicea:

> *3:14 "These things says the Amen, the Faithful and True Witness, the Beginning of the creation of God:"*

Like John, we are captivated by the vision of Jesus and want some day to be like Him. John wrote earlier in 1 John 3: 2-3;

> *"Beloved, now we are children of God; and it has not yet been revealed what we shall be, but we know that when He is revealed, we shall be like Him, for we shall see Him as He is and everyone who has this hope in Him purifies himself, just as He is pure."*

Sometimes the Book of Revelation interprets the symbols for us. When it does we are aided in understanding the nature of the imagery used in other places that aren't interpreted. In verse 20, the interpretation of the first vision begins. He says,

> *"The mystery of the seven stars which you saw in My right hand, and the seven golden lampstands: The seven stars are the angels of the seven churches, and the seven lampstands which you saw are the seven churches."*

Why do you think the church would look like a lamp stand? It is because the church is giving off a light to the world. Jesus says in Matthew chapter 5,

> *"You are the light of the world. A city that is set on a hill cannot be hidden. Nor do they light a lamp and put it under a basket, but on a lampstand, and it gives light to all who are in the house."*

These candlesticks indicate that the church is the light of the world.

The idea of seven churches in the Jewish mind was the sum of four, a number that represented earthly or physical things, plus the number three, which represented the God head - God the Father, God the Son and God the Holy Spirit. So, taking all spiritual things and all physical things you get the totality of all things. When John sees seven lamp stands, he is not just counting but looking at all the churches that exist as the light of the world.

There are also seven stars that represent angels. The word angel means messenger. There was an angel for each church; seven angels, seven stars, seven candlesticks and seven churches. Is there an angel for the church where you worship? From the book of Revelation, I would conclude there is, since seven is that complete number representing all the churches that exist.

REVELATION - CHAPTER 2 AND 3

At the end of chapter 1, John is instructed to write letters to the seven city churches that are in Asia Minor. Chapters 2 and 3 record these letters. The seven city churches that are addressed in the order that they are given form a geographic clockwise circle about 90 miles in diameter. These cities are actual cities, but can represent the spiritual state of the church in many different cultures. Cities have personalities that affect the church. Some cities are rural with farm country while some cities are technical and scientific. The letters for each church, when compared, show great similarity in form in spite of the diversity that the churches represent.

Ephesus, for instance, was a seaport town where there was abundant commerce and many people traveling. Varied nationalities were present. There was a great temple erected to a goddess named Dianna. This city was prone to idolatry.

Smyrna was also a seaport town. Fifty miles to the north of that was the city of Pergamos. It was the capital city of Asia, so it would have government buildings and government officials. Thirty miles to the southeast of Pergamos as you turn the circle and start to the south, you come to Thyatira. Thyatira had a military academy. It would likely be a town that was very structured and formal, full of warfare and warfare teaching. The next city of Sardis, thirty miles to the southeast, was the capital city of an area called Lydia. It was a town of manufacturing and production. The city of Philadelphia, about forty miles to the southeast, was an agricultural center for growing grapes and producing wine. The seventh city is Laodicea, forty five miles southeast of Philadelphia and ninety miles east of Ephesus. Laodicea had a medical school and taught many of the doctors of the area.

The beginning of each letter is the salutation. When we write a letter, we put the greeting to the one written at the top and sign it at the bottom. The custom of that day was to put the greeting at the top and then immediately sign the letter. It is like getting email. When you get email, the one addressed and the sender are at the very top of the message. The chart below compares the salutations to each of the seven churches.

Ephesus	Smyrna	Pergamos	Thyatira	Sardis	Philadelphia	Laodicea
(2:1)To the angel of the church of Ephesus write,	(2:8)And to the angel of the church in Smyrna write,	(2:12)And to the angel of the church in Pergamos write,	(2:18)And to the angel of the church in Thyatira write,	(3:1)And to the angel of the church in Sardis write,	(3:7)And to the angel of the church in Philadelphia write,	(3:14)And to the angel of the church of the Laodiceans write,

The letters then continue with the name of the sender. As we have already noted in the discussion of chapter 1, the identification of the sender is a repetition of the seven elements of the vision of Jesus in chapter 1. These descriptions introduce Jesus as the author of each letter.

Ephesus	Smyrna	Pergamos	Thyatira	Sardis	Philadelphia	Laodicea
(2:1)These things says He who holds the seven stars in His right hand, who walks in the midst of the seven golden lampstands:	*(2:8)These things says the First and the Last, who was dead, and came to life:*	*(2:12)These things says He who has the sharp two-edged sword:*	*(2:18)These things says the Son of God, who has eyes like a flame of fire, and His feet like fine brass:*	*(3:1)These things says He who has the seven Spirits of God and the seven stars:*	*(3:7)These things says He who is holy, He who is true, He who has the key of David, He who opens and no one shuts, and shuts and no one opens:*	*(3:14)These things says the Amen, the Faithful and True Witness, the Beginning of the creation of God:*

The third element in the formation of the letters is very personal. It reflects Jesus' evaluation of the congregation. When I get up in the morning, I get dressed to go to work and meet my wife Carolyn downstairs where she gives me the once over. Usually, I have broken a style rule, and have to make a trip back upstairs to change. We have a tendency to observe and be critical. As Jesus holds the seven stars in his hands and he walks among the seven candlesticks, He observes each church and has John write down what He sees. Jesus evaluates their spiritual condition and the things which affect each church. For example, in chapter 2 and verse 2, Jesus observes the church at Ephesus and says,

> *"I know your works, your labor, your patience, and that you cannot bear those who are evil. And you have tested those who say they are apostles and are not, and have found them liars; and you have persevered and have patience, and have labored for My name's sake and have not become weary."*

This is an observation of praise. Ephesus, you are doing some things right. You are checking out what people say. You are checking their pedigree. You are checking to see if they are really apostles or not and you are finding that some of them are not.

Ephesus	Smyrna	Pergamos	Thyatira	Sardis	Philadelphia	Laodicea
(2:2)I know your works, your labor, your patience, and that you cannot bear those who are evil. And you have tested those who say they are apostles and are not, and have found them liars; and you have persevered and have patience, and have labored for My name's sake and have not become weary.	*(2:9)I know your works, tribulation, and poverty (but you are rich);*	*(2:13)I know your works, and where you dwell, where Satan's throne is. And you hold fast to My name, and did not deny My faith even in the days in which Antipas was My faithful martyr, who was killed among you, where Satan dwells.*	*(2:19)I know your works, love, service, faith, and your patience; and as for your works, the last are more than the first.*	*(3:1)I know your works, that you have a name that you are alive, but you are dead. (3:2)Be watchful, and strengthen the things which remain, that are ready to die,*	*(3:8)I know your works. See, I have set before you an open door, and no one can shut it; for you have a little strength, have kept My word, and have not denied My name.*	*(3:15)I know your works,*

There were marks of an apostle. Those marks are described in Acts chapter 1. We can see the miracles that the apostles were able to perform to confirm the word. There were people who were posing as apostles. Recently the news reported the discovery of the gospel according to Judas. You may not realize that this is just one of many gospels that were written in the first few centuries after Jesus lived. It was a very popular thing to write a gospel about Jesus. Since most of them are fiction, how do you tell the difference between truth and fiction? You test them. That is what Ephesus was doing in the first century. They were testing the so called apostles personally and they were doing it well. Look across the row in the above chart and you will find the observations about the other six churches. For the church in Smyrna, Jesus observed,

> *"I know your works, tribulation, and poverty (but you are rich)."*

Jesus said I can see you are struggling. I can see that the city has economic problems, but you are personally rich. In this section of the letters, Jesus is describing the good things about each of the churches.

The observations about each church are good until you arrive at Laodicea. There Jesus says,

> *"I know your works."*

He has observed Laodicea and He does not have anything good to say. For the others, Jesus has something good to say. For Thyatira, He says,

> *"I know your works, love, service, faith, and your patience; and as for your works, the last are more than the first."*

For Sardis He says,

> *"I know your works, that you have a name that you are alive, but you are dead. Be watchful, and strengthen the things which remain."*

This section of the letters is about the good things Jesus observes about these churches.

In the fourth division of each letter, Jesus notes the problems that have arisen in the churches.

Ephesus	Smyrna	Pergamos	Thyatira	Sardis	Philadelphia	Laodicea
(2:4)Nevertheless I have this against you, that you have left your first love	*(2:9) and I know the blasphemy of those who say they are Jews and are not, but are a synagogue of Satan.*	*(2:14)But I have a few things against you, because you have there those who hold the doctrine of Balaam, who taught Balak to put a stumbling block before the children of Israel, to eat things sacrificed to idols, and to commit sexual immorality.(2:15) Thus you also have those who hold the doctrine of the Nicolaitans, which thing I hate.*	*(2:20)Never the less I have a few things against you, because you allow that woman Jezebel, who calls herself a prophetess, to teach and seduce My servants to commit sexual immorality and eat things sacrificed to idols.*	*(3:2) for I have not found your works perfect before God.*	*(3:9)Indeed I will make those of the synagogue of Satan, who say they are Jews and are not, but lie— indeed I will make them come and worship before your feet, and to know that I have loved you.*	*(3:15) that you are neither cold nor hot. I could wish you were cold or hot. (3:16)So then, because you are lukewarm, and neither cold nor hot, I will vomit you out of My mouth. (3:17)Because you say, 'I am rich, have become wealthy, and have need of nothing'—and do not know that you are wretched, miserable, poor, blind, and naked*

Jesus says to Ephesus,

"Nevertheless I have this against you, that you have left your first love."

What Jesus uses here is a technique that is used and taught today for constructive criticism. If you are going to be critical of somebody, the first thing you should do is find something good to say about them. When I was in Toastmasters years ago, we would critique speeches that people would givewhen learning how to make better speeches. One of the techniques they taught us was called the sandwich method. To be critical of a speaker, the first thing you must do is say something good about their speech. Afterward, you could offer your criticism and then follow up with something good. It is like the meat in-between two slices of bread so it was called the sandwich method. It is a very important technique since criticism and negativity can produce discouragement. It also helps you as the one who is going to be critical to be required to observe something good. Jesus, in the Sermon on the Mount, says

"Blessed are the pure in heart, for they shall see God."

If you are not seeing God when you look around, then there is something wrong with your heart. It is important that you work on your own heart. Jesus demonstrates this principle by pointing out the good things before he points out the things that need correcting.

This section of each letter is the place where we would focus to study the problems in each church. There is a tendency to accentuate the negative. It is amazing how often gospel meetings concentrate on everything that is wrong with the church. Have you ever heard a sermon about what is right with the church? It would be worthwhile to hear one of those.

To the church in Ephesus, Jesus observes that He knows how they have been testing apostles and cannot bear to be in the presence of evil. They were not allowing evil to enter in. They were stern and strict; but, in their sternness and their strictness, they had left their first love. Paul wrote in Ephesians 4:16 that love is the glue that binds the church together. When you can observe someone and find something good about them, it reflects upon the love that you have for that person. Jesus says that Ephesus had left their first love. They had forgotten what it was like to be lost and then saved. They had forgotten what it was like to have their sins forgiven. As I grow older, I realize how easy it is to be critical and how hard it is to love. That was the problem with the church of Ephesus. They were strict and were testing everything as they should, but in so doing, they had forgotten to love. They had left their first love; the love of Jesus Christ and what he had done for them. They had forgotten how their sins had been forgiven and had forgotten to be merciful in their judgments.

To Smyrna Jesus critiques that there are people who are the messengers of Satan in their congregation who are persecuting them. To the city of Pergamos Jesus notes that they hold the

29

doctrine of Balaam and the doctrine of the Nicolaitans. Jesus hates them to be drawn away from the gospel.

There is a tendency in people to write down what they believe. Some churches recite what they call the Apostle's creed as a statement of what they believe. We try to encapsulate what we believe in a few words and say I believe this and everything else I do not. As a boy growing up, I learned that the church of Christ did not have a creed except the Bible. Because I know how fallible I am at trying to write things down and how fallible the human language is at trying to convey it, I need for the Holy Spirit to do that for me. That is why I trust in the scriptures. I need no other authority than the scriptures. I need no other way to look at God's word except God's word itself.

Jesus says that Pergamos has people teaching different doctrines. You have people majoring on areas like fornication or eating things offered to idols. There were lots of questions in the first century because of a blending of Jews and Gentiles and many different cultures coming together. The council of Jerusalem in Acts Chapter 15 was called to bring peace between those Jewish and Gentile Christians. There was a lot of adjustment that was occurring, and this had become a problem in the city of Pergamos. This capital city had people coming in from all over that region who were representatives and senators. These people were generally highly educated and had the tendency to use human wisdom and logic to destroy themselves while ignoring the simplicity that is in the gospel.

Sardis, I have not found your works perfect before God. You are a dead church. Philadelphia is a faithful church. Jesus says that He will make those who say they are Jews and are not come and worship before their feet. They would come to know that Jesus loved the faithful of Philadelphia. He does not have any criticism of Philadelphia whose name means the city of brotherly love.

Finally, He observes that Laodicea is lukewarm. Jesus would prefer that they were either hot or cold. Because they were lukewarm, Jesus found them distasteful and He would spew the out of His mouth."

We have observed that the first section of each letter was the introduction to the church. The next section was the salutation followed by the positive observations and then the negative observations that would need correcting.

The next section of each letter is a call to repentance. Repentance is something that we all need to be doing. We never get to a point in our Christian lives that we do not need to repent. Surprisingly, the closer you get to Jesus, the more you need to repent. Preachers ought to be repenting more. Elders ought to be repenting even more because they are getting closer in their walk to that perfect example of Jesus Christ. Because the path grows narrower, elders need more corrections. Of whom more is given, more is expected. The babe in Christ begins the journey to God starts on a pretty wide open road, but, as his understanding grows, he discovers more and more that he needs to change in his life. Jesus calls us to repentance. Notice that Smyrna and Philadelphia are empty in this section. These were two churches that had very little negative said about them.

Ephesus	Smyrna	Pergamos	Thyatira	Sardis	Philadelphia	Laodicea
(2:5)Remember therefore from where you have fallen; repent and do the first works, or else I will come to you quickly and remove your lampstand from its place— unless you repent.		*(2:16)Repent, or else I will come to you quickly and will fight against them with the sword of My mouth.*	*(2:21)And I gave her time to repent of her sexual immorality, and she did not repent. (2:22) Indeed I will cast her into a sickbed, and those who commit adultery with her into great tribulation, unless they repent of their deeds. (2:23) I will kill her children with death, and all the churches shall know that I am He who searches the minds and hearts. And I will give to each one of you according to your works.*	*(3:3)Remember therefore how you have received and heard; hold fast and repent. Therefore if you will not watch, I will come upon you as a thief, and you will not know what hour I will come upon you.*		*(3:18)I counsel you to buy from Me gold refined in the fire, that you may be rich; and white garments, that you may be clothed, that the shame of your nakedness may not be revealed; and anoint your eyes with eye salve, that you may see. (3:19) As many as I love, I rebuke and chasten. Therefore be zealous and repent.*

In the sixth section of each letter, Jesus compliments those of each church who are repenting and seeking the Lord. For instance, to Sardis He says,

> *"Thou hast a few names even in Sardis which have not defiled their garments; and they shall walk with me in white: for they are worthy."*

Blessed are those that are not succumbing to evil.

31

Ephesus	Smyrna	Pergamos	Thyatira	Sardis	Philadelphia	Laodicea
(2:6)But this you have, that you hate the deeds of the Nicolaitans, which I also hate.	*(2:10)Do not fear any of those things which you are about to suffer. Indeed, the devil is about to throw some of you into prison, that you may be tested, and you will have tribulation ten days. Be faithful until death, and I will give you the crown of life.*		*(2:24)Now to you I say, and to the rest in Thyatira, as many as do not have this doctrine, who have not known the depths of Satan, as they say, I will put on you no other burden. (2:25) But hold fast what you have till I come.*	*(3:4)You have a few names even in Sardis who have not defiled their garments; and they shall walk with Me in white, for they are worthy.*	*(3:10)Because you have kept My command to persevere, I also will keep you from the hour of trial which shall come upon the whole world, to test those who dwell on the earth. (3:11) Behold, I am coming quickly! Hold fast what you have, that no one may take your crown.*	*(3:20)Behold, I stand at the door and knock. If anyone hears My voice and opens the door, I will come in to him and dine with him, and he with Me.*

In the seventh section, Jesus makes promises of perseverance.:

He provides a promise of what is going to be provided for those who overcome. There are several ideas about what this means. One thought is that he that overcomes is everybody who believes. There are religious groups that teach the idea of once you are saved, you are always going to be saved. The second approach is that only the obedient faithful would be those that would overcome and that salvation would be lost to those that did not overcome the evils of their lives. The third idea is that only the obedient faithful would overcome and the others that did not overcome would have reward lost. They would still be saved, but some reward would be lost. 1 Corinthians Chapter 3 talks about being saved as though by fire, and we will spend time studying these thoughts in a later chapter. Which one of these ideas fit? Which ever we choose, it is certain that there is a responsibility of the Christian to overcome and it will not be effortless.

Ephesus	Smyrna	Pergamos	Thyatira	Sardis	Philadelphia	Laodicea
(2:7)To him who overcomes I will give to eat from the tree of life, which is in the midst of the Paradise of God.	(2:11)He who overcomes shall not be hurt by the second death.	(2:17)To him who overcomes I will give some of the hidden manna to eat. And I will give him a white stone, and on the stone a new name written which no one knows except him who receives it.	(2:26)And he who overcomes, and keeps My works until the end, to him I will give power over the nations— (2:27) He shall rule them with a rod of iron; They shall be dashed to pieces like the potter's vessels'— as I also have received from My Father; (2:28) and I will give him the morning star.	(3:5)He who overcomes shall be clothed in white garments, and I will not blot out his name from the Book of Life; but I will confess his name before My Father and before His angels.	(3:12)He who overcomes, I will make him a pillar in the temple of My God, and he shall go out no more. I will write on him the name of My God and the name of the city of My God, the New Jerusalem, which comes down out of heaven from My God. And I will write on him My new name.	(3:21)To him who overcomes I will grant to sit with Me on My throne, as I also overcame and sat down with My Father on His throne.

Jesus then encourages the listeners to really hear. He writes,

"He who has an ear, let him hear what the Spirit says to the churches."

Ephesus	Smyrna	Pergamos	Thyatira	Sardis	Philadelphia	Laodicea
(2:7)He who has an ear, let him hear what the Spirit says to the churches.	(2:11)He who has an ear, let him hear what the Spirit says to the churches.	(2:17)He who has an ear, let him hear what the Spirit says to the churches.	(2:29)He who has an ear, let him hear what the Spirit says to the churches.	(3:6)He who has an ear, let him hear what the Spirit says to the churches.	(3:13)He who has an ear, let him hear what the Spirit says to the churches.	(3:22)He who has an ear, let him hear what the Spirit says to the churches.

All of the letters have the identical statement. It is through the power of preaching that God chose to save those who believe. However, Paul in Acts Chapter 26 when discussing trying to preach to the Jews, describes them as having ears that are fat. Have you ever been accused of having fat ears? My daughter Renee and I were looking at some pictures recently. We had a picture of Renee when she was hardly a year old at her first Christmas. She was sitting on the floor playing with one of her Christmas toys. Renee called her son, John Nicks, over and said to him, "Look at my picture when I was just a year old." Her son replied, and said "All I see are two ears with a baby hanging on them." Renee inherited my big ears. She keeps them covered up now with hair but nonetheless, she has big ears. But does she hear with those ears? Sometimes people do not want to hear what is being said. Renee had her little poodle dog in the yard. The dog is 16 years old and is feeble. It is hard of hearing and almost blind. It was running off to the edge of the yard and Renee called for it. Somebody spoke up and said, "Oh that dog is deaf." Renee's husband Jay said, "Oh no, it has selective hearing and hears what it wants to. Call it to supper if you do not believe it." All of us have a certain amount of selective hearing and so it was with these churches. Jesus says to the churches, "He who has an ear, let him hear what the Spirit says to the churches." Sometimes, the Lord brings us to places where we are forced to hear but we will just not listen.

REVELATION – CHAPTER 4

Chapter 4 of Revelation is either the second vision of John or a continuation of the first vision that started in chapter 1 when John first saw Jesus. Either way, John changes position in this chapter. In chapter 1, he was on the Isle of Patmos in exile. It was the Lord's Day and he was in the Spirit. As a result, he saw Jesus who dictated to him the letters to the seven churches recorded in chapters 2 and 3. In chapter 4 we are returned to being in the Spirit on the Isle of Patmos on the Lord's Day but are soon ushered into heaven.

In verse 1 John writes, "After these things", referring to the things that occurred in Chapter 1 and the dictating of the letters contained in chapters 2 and 3. John continues,

> *"I looked, and behold, a door standing open in heaven. And the first voice which I heard was like a trumpet speaking with me, saying, 'Come up here, and I will show you things which must take place after this.'"*

Notice that there is a door in Heaven, and that it is open. Revelation 3:20 leads right into this vision of chapter 4 where there was a door, but it was closed.

> *"Behold, I stand at the door and knock. If anyone hears My voice and opens the door, I will come in to him and dine with him, and he with Me."*

This door refers to the door of our heart, the door that would make us receptive to the words of Jesus. If you will open your door, Jesus will come in. However, in chapter 4, the door in Heaven is an open door. A powerful message is being conveyed. God is always waiting for our entry. The door to heaven is open. However, the door to our hearts is sometimes closed. It is our responsibility to open ourselves up to the Lord. The Lord is going to always be open to us. The Lord is just beyond an open door.

In the Old Testament tabernacle, there was a holy place and a most holy place that were separated by a curtain, a door that was always closed. God was in the presence of Israel, but he was behind a door that only the High Priest could enter once a year. When they disassembled the tabernacle to move it from one place to another, they carried the ark from the most holy place on poles and were not allowed to touch it. There was a man named Uzzah who touched the ark and was struck dead. God was not as near in the Old Testament as he is in the New Testament. We are going to learn why in chapter 4.

The welcome to come into God's presence is through the voice that comes to John in verse 1. John notes that the first voice that he heard was like a trumpet. In Chapter 1:10, when John heard the voice of Jesus, it was like a trumpet. Coming into the presence of God is always only with the invitation of Jesus.

As we study the Book of Revelation, we will discover a lot of imagery, things which represent something else. An example is the seven candle sticks representing the seven churches, the seven stars representing the seven angels. This is not my interpretation. This is what Jesus told John they represented. In the best case, we can learn about the imagery from what Jesus says the Revelation means. The next best case in having a real understanding of the imagery is revealed in this verse. John wrote that the first voice which he heard was like a trumpet. It does not say that the voice was a trumpet. It says it was "like" a trumpet. The deduction is that the voice reminded John of a trumpet. It had characteristics of a trumpet. It was not a trumpet, but it reminded him of a trumpet. What is there about a trumpet sound that would make you say it sounded like a trumpet? Was it loud, piercing, and blaring? I would think it might even be musical. The Hebrews would often chant, so perhaps the voice was musically chanting. I think the voice was loud and piercing and there was no doubt that someone important was speaking. Even if you were hard of hearing, you would have heard the sound.

This voice that came from Heaven through the open door invited John to come up here. The last chapter of Revelation also ends with an invitation where Jesus offers that the bride and the spirit say come. Obviously, God wants us to come along with him. He has opened the door. He has trumpeted an invitation and He wants you to come. We are all going to come up. In the book of 1 Thessalonians when the trumpet sounds on that last day, we are all going to rise to meet him in the air. The dead first and then those who are living will be changed and will all rise to meet him in the air. As I imagine the trumpet on the last day, it is going to say, come on up! "Hallelujah Anyway!"

The Revelator begins this vision wanting us with Him so He can reveal to us the things which are to come. This does not exclude the fact that Jesus has already told John that he is going to prophecy about the things that were and the things that are and the things that will be. Oftentimes, we think of prophecy as foretelling the future, but prophecy is much more than that. Prophecy means being a spokesman for God. A prophet as a spokesman for God tells about the things in the past, the present and the future. Moses is referred to as a prophet, and yet Moses spoke mostly about things that had occurred thousands of years before he was born. It was revealed to him through inspiration concerning the creation, and the stories of the patriarchs. Because of the prophecy of Moses it is revealed to us the history of mankind under the tutelage of God. The prophet John, as he was to prophecy the things that he had seen in these visions, was to prophesy about the past, the present and the future. However, John, like us, is probably very interested in the things that will be. Jesus promises to reveal the things that will take place after this. This is a promise. If you come up here, I will show you the things that are going to take place.

In verse 2 John reports,

> *"Immediately, I was in the spirit."*

John had already stated in Chapter 1 that he was in the Spirit on the Lord's Day. Is it possible to be in the Spirit and then be in the spirit? I think so. "I was in the Spirit on the Lord's Day," in Chapter 1, speaks of the fact that John was in a worshipful state; that he had an attitude of seeking God. That God's Spirit was working with his spirit. However, in Chapter 4, it says, "Immediately, I was in the spirit", and then, "Behold a throne set in Heaven." John has been transported. Being in the spirit here is leaving the physical state that would limit him from entering into Heaven. The Bible tells us that flesh and blood cannot inherit the Kingdom of God. This mortal must put on immortality. The idea of being immediately in the spirit could be that John was transformed into a spiritual state that could meet the Lord in Heaven. John was able to pass through the door and enter what we will refer to as the throne room of God. As he entered that door into the throne room of God, it was not a physical journey. It was a spiritual journey. Immediately, I was in the spirit and behold, a throne set in Heaven and one who sat on that throne. Who is sitting on the throne? You might guess that it was Jesus, but later in chapter 5 we will learn that it is the Father.

And He who sat there was like; there is that word "like" again. That is the reason we have already pointed out the word "like" because we are going to see it a lot. It did not say He was a jasper, but He was "like" a jasper and sardius stone in appearance. There was a rainbow around the throne in an appearance like an emerald. Exodus 28:17-20 says;

> *"And you shall put settings of stones in it, four rows of stones: The first row shall be a sardius, a topaz, and an emerald; this shall be the first row; the second row shall be a turquoise, a sapphire, and a diamond; the third row, a jacinth, an agate, and an amethyst; and the fourth row, a beryl, an onyx, and a jasper. They shall be set in gold settings."*

This reference is describing the breast plate of the Old Testament priests' clothing. It is telling about the tabernacle and the worship area and the clothing that the priest should wear. A breast plate reminds me of military men that have been in a lot of campaigns and they have ribbons of decoration on their uniforms. That is a breast plate in a modern sense. The breast plate of Bible times covered the whole chest so that during a battle or a fight, you could tell friend from foe by the breast plate. Roman soldiers wore a breast plate that had an eagle spread out on it. That was the indicator, the icon, for the nation of Rome. The breast plate of the High Priest was a set of four rows of stones, three stones in each row, or a total of 12 stones. These stones represented the twelve tribes of Israel. Each stone belonged to one of those particular tribes. Also, each of those stones was different to indicate the differences in those tribes. The very first stone mentioned was Sardius. This is the last one that is mentioned in the throne room. The last one mentioned in the breast plate was Jasper. Jasper is the first one mentioned in Revelation. John took the first stone and the last stone of the breastplate and reversed the order of them.

Jasper is a stone that is white. In the Book of Revelation white usually means purity. God will dress you in white robes. Christ is riding on a white horse. The imagery of white is of purity. Who is the purest of all? The resurrected Lord is pure and holy. God is holy. The other stone, the Sardius stone (a ruby), is blood red. The promise and prophecy from the stones that were from the breast plate may have represented prophecy about the coming of Jesus. There was going to have to be a shedding of the blood of Son of God to provide purity. The rainbow that was over the throne is an indicator of the covenant of God. The rainbow was a symbol of an agreement between God and man. In this picture of the throne room the One sitting on the throne provides purity by the blood of the lamb and remembers His promise to His people. White is the color of the Old Covenant and red is the color of the new covenant and the rainbow is the symbol of the covenant.

In verse 4 we read.

> *"Around the throne were twenty-four thrones, and on the thrones I saw twenty-four elders sitting, clothed in white robes; and they had crowns of gold on their heads."*

Recall the discussion on numerology and notice that twenty-four is twelve plus twelve. Also remember that twelve represents organized religion. The idea that the earth represented by four cardinal directions and God represented by three persons multiplied together represents God's interaction with man or religion. We have twelve and twelve or twenty-four elders. Remember there were twelve tribes in the old covenant and twelve apostles in the new covenant. So an elder would represent a leader of organized religion. Each elder has a crown to demonstrate that he is a ruler or leader. We will see this contrast between the covenants often in Revelation. When Judas committed suicide and there remained only eleven apostles, the remaining apostles were interested in getting one more so there would again be twelve. I do not personally believe that the apostles picked the one God would pick because we do not read about Mathias anymore in the Bible. Instead, we read about another one named Paul that was picked by Jesus out of due season. Mathias was chosen by lots, but Paul was chosen by Jesus.

We have a picture representing the covenants that God has had with man in the form of these 24 elders. Being called elders would indicate that they were older. They were wiser and wore crowns upon their heads. They sat on thrones. Jesus promised in the letters that those who were faithful would sit on thrones and rule.

Verse 5 reveals that from the throne proceeded lightning and thundering and voices. Seven lamps of fire were burning before the throne, which are the seven Spirits of God. I cannot imagine coming into the presence of God, but I can imagine a storm with lightning and thunder. Somebody told me when I was a small boy that the thunder rolling through the clouds is the Lord bowling. Every time I hear thunder, it reminds me of the power and majesty of God. That is what John was doing. John had to pick earthly terms to describe what he was seeing and he was sharing that the presence of God was overpowering.

What are these seven Spirits of God? There is only one Holy Spirit. John was a student of the Old Testament. God revealed Himself in the Old Testament. Isaiah 11:2-3 says,

> *"The Spirit of the Lord shall rest upon Him, The Spirit of wisdom and understanding, The Spirit of counsel and might, The Spirit of knowledge and of the fear of the Lord."*

These are seven characteristics of the Spirit. They are going to rest on Him. We see them as pots of fire. I refer you to the interpretive tool of "Put Jesus in it". If you don't understand it, put Jesus in it. Isaiah has prophesied that there are going to be seven qualities of the Spirit that are going to be put upon Jesus. Actually, six qualities plus the Spirit itself makes seven in the Book of Isaiah. We find that Jesus possessed all of these qualities. We are being introduced to Jesus in a lot of different ways. We are being introduced to Jesus by the stones. We are being introduced to Jesus by the seven spirits. In Acts, Chapter 2, when the Holy Spirit was poured out He appeared as tongues of fire. Here we have seven lamps of fire.

In verse 6 John reveals that before the throne there was a sea of glass *like* crystal. You might mistakenly say it is a crystal sea but it was a sea that was *like* crystal. Crystal is shiny, smooth, and reflects light. What John saw is this great image of God on His throne. He is full of light and in front of him is this sea of crystal that is reflecting that great light and the sea is calm. We are reminded of this sea three times in the Book of Revelation. This sea is mentioned also in Revelation 15:2 and 21:1. In 15:2, it is not calm, but is turbulent, full of fire. The third time it is mentioned, it says there is no more sea before the throne of God. It is gone. So, it is crystal, fiery and gone. We will discuss this further in a later chapter.

> *"And in the midst of the throne, and around the throne, were four living creatures full of eyes in front and in back. The first living creature was like a lion, the second living creature like a calf, the third living creature had a face like a man, and the fourth living creature was like a flying eagle. The four living creatures, each having six wings, were full of eyes around and within. And they do not rest day or night, saying: Holy, holy, holy, Lord God Almighty, Who was and is and is to come!"*

In these verses, we are introduced to four creatures. The word creature in the Bible is a translation of a word that means soul, living souls, created beings of God. Some have thought that these four living creatures are cherubim (an order of angels).

They have six wings. Where would God put six wings? In Ezekiel 1:1-14, Ezekiel sees these four living creatures. He describes them in similar fashion. He describes them as having four faces; one face like a lion, one like an ox, one like a man and one like an eagle. I suppose this was a calf of an ox. For the wings, Ezekiel describes that they had four sides and never had to turn. Each of the four sides had a wing and they had two wings to cover their body.

Angels are God's ministers to us. They can see everything that is happening since they have eyes on all sides. They can see in all directions which ever way they move. They look like a lion, calf, man and an eagle. The word "like" is used. What could this possibly mean? I have read all kinds of ideas and I really do not know what it means. However, the lion reminds me of the tribe of Judah from which the Messiah came. He is known as the Lion of Judah. If you do not understand what it is, put Jesus in it. The face of a lion could be representative of the powerful nature of Jesus being of the tribe of Judah. The calf would represent the idea of the service and sacrifice of Jesus. A calf was often sacrificed in the Jewish blood sacrifice. The third one, the man, was likened to the Son of Man in we discussed in chapter 1. Jesus had the appearance of a man. Jesus counted being an equal of God, a thing not to be grasped, but emptied himself and took on the form of a servant and became a man. Hebrews said he was created a little lower than the angels, he became a man. What about the eagle? An eagle has a sharp eye. The eagle is a glorious animal. I am reminded of Isaiah 40:31. Those that wait on the Lord will run and never get tired. They will be lifted up on eagle's wings. One of the prophets talks about how the eagles would train their young to fly and compared that to how God trains us. So, we see Jesus as the great trainer, Jesus, as the one who would lead us. We would be like him. He would protect us and care for us. Remember what Jesus said when he was weeping over Jerusalem?

> *"O Jerusalem, Jerusalem, the one who kills the prophets and stones those who are sent to her! How often I wanted to gather your children together, as a hen gathers her chicks under her wings, but you were not willing!"*

Jesus describes Himself as a bird of protection and saving. I see the living creatures as a reflection of Jesus.

Some have hypothesized that these creatures represent the four gospels. Mathew described the Lion of Judah. Mark revealed the servant characteristics of Jesus. Luke talked about Jesus the man, and John talked about Jesus who had the ability to train and teach. You can make it fit, but it is a stretch.

In verse 9,

> *"Whenever the living creatures give glory and honor and thanks to Him who sits on the throne, who lives forever and ever, the twenty-four elders fall down before Him who sits on the throne and worship Him who lives forever and ever, and cast their crowns before the throne, saying: 'You are worthy, O Lord, To receive glory and honor and power; For You created all things, And by Your will they exist and were created.'"*

God sounds like a great trumpet. God is like a bright light with thundering and lightening coming out of the throne. He is like a great sea of crystal that reflects His glory. All the twenty-four elders with their crowns of gold around them, and we will discover later a multitude of hosts that are gathered around him also. The four living creatures, very strange animals, moving in and around

Him through the throne and in the midst of the throne and in the middle of all this they are crying Holy, Holy, Holy. They worship with the words; You are worthy of glory. You are worthy of honor. You are worthy of thanks. You are worthy of worship. You are worthy because you have power. You are worthy because You are the creator and we bow ourselves. We humble ourselves before You. We take off any crown that might make us feel important and we cast it before the throne because of how much more majestic You are than us.

John paints a beautiful word picture of the glory and the majesty and the power and the greatness of the God whom we serve. Revelation Chapter 4 is a favorite one of mine for the glimpse that it gives us of the Almighty God.

REVELATION – CHAPTER 5

In chapter four, we were introduced to the heavenly place. This vision is from John, who was caught up in heaven, and hence is a vision with a heavenly perspective. It is a vision that is going to be reporting events that are taking place in heaven during the history of the world. I hope this will be obvious when we get to chapter 12 where the nature of the vision changes to observe the same events from an earthly perspective. There John will be recounting the same thing from another vantage point, from another viewpoint in what I have called chronological flashback.

In chapter 5, we are going to see that not only is God the Father who sits upon the throne worthy of being worshiped, but the Lamb (Jesus Christ) is also worthy of being worshiped,. The subtitle for chapter 5 could be "Worthy is the Lamb." Songs have been written with words taken from this chapter to remind us that Jesus is worthy. Remember that we have commented already that if you do not understand something in the Bible, try putting Jesus in it. The Bible is about Jesus. So, as you study, keep Jesus in the middle of things and it will bring enlightenment. This chapter reveals that no one can open the events of the past, the present or the future except the Lamb who is worthy to open what has been sealed.

> *"And I saw in the right hand of Him who sat on the throne a scroll written inside and on the back, sealed with seven seals."*

The word for scroll here is the Greek word biblion. It is the same as the English word, Bible. It is translated as scroll because a book would have been a scroll in the time of Christ. They wrote on parchment. They connected the parchments together and rolled it into a scroll. Writing material was very expensive in that day and would have been written on the front and on the back. They would not have wasted any of the parchment.

Later in the Book of Revelation, in chapter 20 for instance, the translators translate the same Greek word as books. It could have just as well said the scrolls are opened. The reason I bring this up is so you understand there is nothing mystical about this scroll. It is a book that God has written. I believe from what I read here that this book contains things that were hidden throughout the ages. The scroll contains the mystery of God that Paul speaks of in Ephesians 1. The Hebrew writer talks of those who went before us who did not understand the promises and the faith in which they believed, but that it had been revealed to us. Daniel, in his visions was told to close the books and to not reveal what had been written in them. We discover in this chapter the reason they could not be revealed is because Christ had not yet been revealed.

This scroll is sealed with seven seals. I do not understand how this is done exactly. As this vision unfolds you will see one seal at a time coming off this book and as these seals come off, various things are revealed that are written in the book. As these seals are removed, portions of the book could be opened. If it were a scroll, I cannot imagine how you could seal it with seven external visible seals and still open it partially. If you could, some of the seals would be inside and you would not see them at the start. I'm not able to imagine exactly what this book looked like. However, that is just the engineer in me and really has no bearing on the vision of John.

However, it is a book that was divided into seven parts; seven chapters if you prefer. Each chapter had a seal on it; a seal that kept it from being open. Daniel 12:4 and Ezekiel 2: 9-10 also discuss this sealed up book. This is the book that God had in those days which could not yet be revealed.

Then, I saw a strong angel proclaiming with a loud voice,

> *"Who is worthy to open the scroll and to loose its seals?"*

We find that there is a need on the part of God in His Revelation to have someone who is worthy of providing us the answers to the questions that we need. John, as he sees the vision, is inspired to talk about this angel as a strong angel. He did not talk about him being a fast angel. He did not talk about him being a flying angel. He talked about him being a strong angel. Why do you suppose he would have thought about the characteristic of strength in this context? Perhaps he was a guard, keeping someone from opening the scroll who was not worthy. Perhaps it could be that just strength alone wouldn't allow one to open the book.

Strength alone does not make you worthy. We place a lot of importance on being strong. When I was growing up my daddy told me that boys do not cry. I had to learn better about that. However, he told me to be strong and some of my early married life I spent being strong, when I should have been me. Those were lessons I learned that show that strength is not always the key. In revealing the will of God, it is not strength and might. God is not interested in strength alone. He could force every one of us to be robots and do exactly what he wants us to do, and yet, he chooses to not do that. He has the power and the majesty and the might to put anything in order, but he does not. And so, it isn't strength and power that reveals the will of God. This angel represents the strength that was guarding the scroll from being opened or perhaps he was an angel unable to open the scroll just because he was mighty.

No one in Heaven or on Earth or under the Earth was able to open or to look at the scroll. John has just been called up into Heaven. We see the heavenly realm filled with the twenty-four elders and four living creatures and the heavenly host and all of the angels. Among all of them there was no one worthy to open the book. On the Earth there are Paul and John and the apostles who were given the Holy Spirit so they could reveal the word of God, but they cannot open this book. It is not possible for any of those great patriarchs who lived on the earth to open the book. Daniel had to cry because he had to leave the book sealed up that he had seen. He could not reveal it. Ezekiel saw the book sealed up. There was no prophet that could reveal what was in this book. They could only see shadows of it. Under the Earth there was no one worthy. Later, we will learn this may be death and Hades. In Greek thought there was something called the underworld. It was the place where dead spirits lived. So no one alive, no one dead, no one physical, no one spiritual was worthy to open the scroll.

In verse four John reveals that he wept much because no one was found worthy to open or to read the scrolls. No one was worthy. What was required? It was not strength. It was not where we live. It was not kind of creation we are. It does not have to do with whether we are alive or dead. No one was worthy and John wept.

One of the elders said to me, "Do not weep." Behold, the Lion of the tribe of Judah, the root of David has prevailed to open the scroll and to loose the seven seals. There are two references to this that we should consider. One is in the Book of Genesis and the other is in the Book of Isaiah. The one in Genesis refers to the Tribe of Judah. Jesus was of the Tribe of Judah. Judah is the tribe of the lion. The lion is regal, royal, the king of the jungle. Isaiah 11:1 and 10 is also about the Lion of Judah. He is of the root of David. In 1 Samuel, David wanted to build God a temple. God refused David, but promised that his Son would build the temple. Solomon, David's son, thought that meant him so he built a temple to God. I think Solomon was mistaken. I believe God was referring to His son of the lineage of David who would build the temple. Jesus said to tear down this temple and He would build it back in three days. In 1 Corinthians 3, we come to understand the temple Jesus built was His resurrected body so that when we are in Jesus we are the temple of God, a temple not made with hands. The people who are looking for Jesus to come back and build a physical temple fail to realize the real temple is already built.

In verse six, John wrote,

> *"And I looked, and behold, in the midst of the throne and of the four living creatures, and in the midst of the elders, stood a Lamb as though it had been slain, having seven horns and seven eyes, which are the seven Spirits of God sent out into all the earth."*

This lion, the root of David, appears to John as a lamb. I cannot think of anything meeker than a lamb and anything stronger than a mighty angel, but it is the meek Lamb that is able to open the book. The Lamb is worthy because He has been slain. The Lamb was unique. It had seven horns. Horns in the Book of Revelation are an indication of authority. The authority figure of the church is Jesus. In Mathew 28, Jesus noted that all authority has been given to Him in heaven and on earth. If somebody has all of the authority, then no one else has any authority. The authority in the Kingdom of God belongs to Jesus. In the vision of Daniel 7:24 there were ten horns and these horns are described as being kings. The scriptures refer to Jesus as the King of Kings. Seven here indicates complete. Jesus is the complete King, the only King, and the Supreme Potentate. God had chosen in Him for the fullness of God to dwell bodily. Jesus the Lamb that was slain is the only one who is worthy to open the book.

The Lamb has seven eyes. We noticed that the four living creatures had eyes all over them. Eyes front and back, eyes facing every direction so they could see where they were going. The Lamb had seven eyes. In other words, the Lamb is all knowing and all seeing. Jesus has the complete ability to see and understand. Jesus has walked in our shoes and knows what it is like to be us. My Jesus knows. Jesus the Lamb is portrayed with seven eyes.

Jesus took the scroll out of the right hand of the one who sat on the throne. He took the book from the hand of God because He is worthy to open it. The Hebrew writer says it is not possible for the blood of bulls and goats to take away sin. We were bought with the price of the precious blood of the Lamb of God, a Lamb without a spot, without blemish. The Lamb is the only one who is worthy. He is the only one without sin who could die and satisfy the justice of God for each of us who do sin. He is worthy. He is worthy to reveal the things in the book. As the scroll is opened it is going to tell about God's plan for mankind, and how the Lamb is the key to understanding that plan.

When Jesus had taken the scroll, the living creatures and the twenty-four elders fell down before the Lamb, each having a harp and golden bowls of incense, which are the prayers of the saints. This is the same thing that happened in Chapter 4. The twenty-four elders bowed down. They took their crowns off indicating that they were servants of the One who sat on the throne.

> *"All things were made through Him, and without Him nothing was made that was made. In Him was life, and the life was the light of men. And the light shines in the darkness, and the darkness did not comprehend it."*

The elders had harps and golden bowls full of incense. People will use this to justify musical instruments in church because there are harps in heaven; but what are these harps? You do not have to wonder. They are not four stringed instruments like ancient harps. They are not even five string instruments like my banjo or a six string instrument like your guitar or hundreds of strings like a modern harp. They are the prayers of the saints. What is it that makes sweet music to God? What is it that is a sweet smelling savor and incense to God? It is our prayers, our communication with God; our desire to talk with him. I love it when my children come and want to sit and talk with me. They are all grown. They have lives of their own, but sometimes they come around to just talk. It is so wonderful. I can imagine how God, who created all of us, relishes the fact that we love him enough to want to talk to him. The prayers of the saints are sweet to God.

> *"You are worthy to take the scroll, and to open its seals; for You were slain, and have redeemed us to God by Your blood out of every tribe and tongue and people and nation."*

So now, we know why He is worthy. It is because He is the slain Lamb. He is the One who loved enough to give His life. He is the one who laid down His life for his friends. He has made us kings and priests to our God. We shall reign on the earth with Him.

Then I looked and heard the voices of many angels around the throne, the living creatures and the elders and the number of them was 10,000 times 10,000. That is one billion; 10,000 times 10,000 and thousands of thousands. Do you suppose that these are literal numbers? Did John count them all? What is John expressing to you with that number? There were a lot of them. As he looked , every where he could look, every where he could see, there were people who were singing a new song with a loud voice saying that the Lamb is worthy to receive power and riches, wisdom, strength, honor and glory and blessings.

Those are the words in the song we talked about at the beginning of this lesson. Every creature who is in heaven and on the earth and under the earth and such as are in the sea are singing. John heard all of them saying blessings and honoring and glory and power be to Him who sits on the throne and to the Lamb forever and ever.

This reminds me of that day when Jesus made his triumphant entry into Jerusalem on the back of a donkey. All of the people came and lay down palm fronds in front of him saying, Hosanna, King of the Jews. Some asked Jesus to stop the crowd from saying that. Jesus told them if they stopped even the rocks would cry out. The Psalmist talks of the trees clapping their hands and the mountains singing. If you have ever taken a long stroll somewhere in the woods far away from people and just listened to the sounds of nature, you can imagine all of those things reaching out their voices. Every creature in the sea, the porpoises and the whales and all of the animals that are in the sea, every person that is above the earth, on the earth and in the earth beginning to sing praise and saying,

> *"Worthy is the Lamb who was slain to receive power and riches and wisdom, and strength and honor and glory and blessing!"*

We are going to see that one day. We will see it when that trumpet sounds and everyone is resurrected to meet the Lord in the air. Every knee will bow and every tongue will confess. It is God's plan to bring glory to His Son who is worthy to open the book; and the four living creatures said amen.

> *"And the twenty-four elders fell down and worshiped Him who lives forever and ever."*

Chapters 4 and 5 of the Book of Revelation go together and introduce us to the Father and to the Son. The Father, by His very being is worthy of worship, and the Son because of His sacrifice is worthy to unveil, to remove the shadows, to turn the light on to the plans of God so that we can see and understand.

REVELATION – CHAPTERS 6, 7, AND 8

The vision we started in chapters 4 and 5 continues in chapters 6, 7, and 8 with the opening of the seven seals. The vision is from the throne room of God and has a heavenly perspective. From Jesus' comments in chapter 1 we learn this heavenly perspective is of the history of God's creation from beginning to end (the things that were and are and will be). This is in opposition to the interpretive approaches to Revelation discussed earlier. However, the flashback approach that we are proposing will show that the visions reveal God's planning for all the history of the world. This history revealed in the vision is God's heavenly architecture that He laid down from the foundation of the world as to how things would transpire. This mystery of God hidden from the ages is now able to be revealed because of the victory of Jesus.

This lesson covers chapter 6, 7 and the first three verses of chapter 8. In Chapter 8, the seventh seal is opened, and there are seven trumpets revealed. The seven trumpets that complete the rest of this first vision from heaven are in the remaining verses of chapters 8 through 11.

As we take a quick overview of the seven seals, we note that the first four are very similar. Each of the first four seals, when opened reveals a horse with a rider. The horses are different colors and the riders are equipped in different ways. I think of the fifth seal as "How long oh Lord, how long?" These are the words from those who have died for God's cause and want to know the end. I am reminded of the Book of Daniel, where Daniel before the last vision is given to him asked how long it would be. Daniel was in bondage and he wanted to know how long he was going to have to wait. Would freedom be in his lifetime? It is the same question we have today. We have questions about bad things happening to good people and we ask how long is this going to go on. The sixth seal reveals the sealing of the saved; of Israel and all other nations. Then the seventh seal is opened and reveals seven trumpets that will complete God's judgment of the world.

With this overview, let us now study them in greater detail. The first four seals are referred to as the four horseman of the apocalypse. There has been a movie made by that name, which had nothing to do with the Book of Revelation. What is an apocalypse? It is the word revelation in the Greek language. These first four seals reveal four horsemen. The horsemen are riding horses that are different colors. The first seal opens to a white horse. The second seal reveals a red horse. The third seal opens to a black horse and the fourth seal shows us a pale horse. There are four different colored horses and the horseman also look quite different.

With the opening of the first seal, a white horse appears with a rider who sat on him. The rider had a bow and a crown and he went forth to conquer. There is another reference in the Book of Revelation to a white horse. White was a symbol of purity. When we see a bride at a wedding she is adorned in white representing her purity. The Book of Revelation tells us that those around the throne of God are wearing white robes. The white robes have been washed in the blood of the Lamb. In

Revelation 19 we are going to learn that the rider there on the white horse is Jesus. There is no reason to deviate from what Revelation interprets so the first horseman must be Jesus. Remember to always put Jesus into a prophecy to understand it. So this first horseman is Jesus. He has a crown given to him. Jesus is referred to as the Christ which means the anointed one. Anointing was something they did before they crowned the King; and Jesus is named the King of Kings and Lord of Lords. The crown definitely complements that idea that the horseman is Jesus.

He had a bow and a crown and He went forth conquering and to conquer. In those days, a kingdom was owned by a king and the king was anticipated to protect his kingdom. Do you remember the apostles coming to Jesus and asking him when the kingdom would come?" When Jesus was attacked, Peter drew his sword to fight. The apostles thought they would have to fight to win the kingdom. The Jews were concerned about Jesus as one who would be king and turned Him in to the Roman governor, Pilate. Pilate asked him,

> *"Are You the King of the Jews?"*

Jesus responded,

> *"My kingdom is not of this world. If My kingdom were of this world, My servants would fight, so that I should not be delivered to the Jews; but now My kingdom is not from here."*

And so that kingly Jesus was wearing a crown riding on a white horse carrying a bow and going forth to conquer.

The second seal reveals a red horse. Red in the Book of Revelation is also used more than once. The devil is introduced as a red dragon in Revelation 12:3. Red is symbolic of Satan. The red horse represents evil and bloodshed and battle. The rider is Satan. The vision indicates that Satan will take peace from the Earth. What causes unrest and a lack of peace on the earth? Was it not Satan coming and sowing sin in the Garden of Eden? Was it not Satan bringing sin into the world? Jesus, when he was on this earth said,

> *"Peace I give to you. My peace I leave with you."*

Paul said that he had a peace that passed understanding indicating that being out of Christ is never peaceful.

The scripture did not say that Satan had the power to take away peace. However, it said the power was given to him. Any power that Satan has is a power that is given to him. In the story of Job in the Old Testament, Satan at every turn had to ask God how far he could go and God granted him liberties for the proving of the faith of Job. In the Book of Job, we see the meaning of this battle that goes on between right and wrong. In the Book of Revelation, the vision reveals that God created all things and just as He created good, much to many people's surprise, He also created evil. All things were made by Him. He created Satan. He knew that this battle between good and evil was going to happen. This heavenly vision views the creation not in terms of planets and earth and sun, but in terms of the struggle between right and wrong. It is viewed as the battle between the man of sin and man of righteousness.

The third seal reveals a black horse. If you were to go to court, you would expect to see the judge dressed in black. Just as purity is represented by white and evil is represented by red, so we find that justice and judgment is represented by black. The white horse and horseman crowned with a crown is Jesus Christ and He is given authority over all of that is good. Satan is shown on a red horse doing battle with good. The rider of the white horse and the rider of the red horse will kill one another. In Genesis 3:15, we are told that from the foundation of the earth, God had planned that they would kill one another. However, the killing of Jesus would not be fatal but the killing of Satan would. Satan was bruised on his head, a mortal wound, while the seed of woman (Jesus Christ) would be bruised on his heel, a non-mortal wound. The third seal reveals the judgment between good and evil. It is required that we make a choice between good or evil. Jesus tells us that you cannot serve God material things. You cannot love one without hating the other. We all have judgment between the two.

When the third seal was opened, the rider on the black horse had a pair of balances in his hand. Balances are used to weigh things, to make a determination, to make a judgment. Even today, scales are the symbol of a judge. The rider had a pair of balances and there was a voice in the midst of the four beasts which said,

> *"A quart of wheat for a denarius, and three quarts of barley for a denarius; and do not harm the oil and the wine."*

There is judgment between wheat and barley while not hurting the oil and the wine, This is indicative of what Jesus taught in the sermon on the Mount when he said that God sends the rain on the just and the unjust. It would be very simple to make a judgment if God would just mark evil. Imagine if you could trust a car salesman who had a white hat and not trust one with a red hat. God could do that. God could mark them if he chose to; but God wants us to make the judgment. God wants us to be able to judge, so He does not mark good and evil. He sends the rain on the just and the unjust. He also sends struggles and problems upon the just and the unjust. That is why bad things happen to good people. That is why good things happen to bad people. It is because the price of oil and wine is protected by this third rider, this judgment rider.

When God created the world, he created everything. He said it was good. Isaiah tells us that God created evil. That means God gave us a choice, a freedom to be like God in our nature. We are able to choose between right and wrong. As God created the choices, He knew there would be a great battle between them from the foundation of the world.

The fourth seal when opened brings forth a pale horse. What is the ultimate outcome of the battle between good and evil portrayed here? The ultimate outcome, Paul tells us in Romans chapter 3 is that all men sin and fall short of the glory of God. When you sin, the wages of sin is death. This fourth rider is named death. Hell followed with him. The word hell there is not the place of punishment. The word in the Greek Bible is Hades. It is the place of the dead. The name of the fourth rider is death and the place of the dead followed him. Power was given unto him over the fourth part of the earth to kill with sword and with hunger and with death and with the beasts of the earth. We do not know how we are going to die and our death may not be directly related to just our sin. When God promised that he would not hurt the oil and wine, He required death come to all men. Hebrew 9:27 says,

> *"And as it is appointed for men to die once, but after this the judgment."*

So the power was given to this rider death over a fourth part of the earth. A large percentage of the living are dying each moment. Every few seconds someone is dying on the earth. A fourth part of the earth is the way it is described here. The fourth may have to do with numerology, since the number four is about earthly things. This is an earthly death and not a spiritual death. We die physically, but there is a second death where we could die spiritually.

John has revealed the picture of the four horsemen from the first four seals. The picture reveals that God has planned to make a creation and to create both good and evil. Good and evil will do battle with each other but there is going to be judgment made between good and evil. The consequence of choosing evil is death and death is going to visit all men because all men sin. God is not partial and judgment is going to fall upon a fourth of the earth.

When the fifth seal was opened, we find under the altar the souls of them who were slain. These are people who have died for the cause of God. Imagine a world that God would create and you might think that God would protect those who are good. This philosophy is in the world today. When we see a disaster or we see an innocent child who dies and we think, well there must not be a God. However, the truth is that God set up the world with choices that has the result that sometimes the righteous would suffer. He demonstrates here in this fifth seal the souls of those of them that were slain for the testimony that they held.

They cried with a loud voice saying,

> *"How long, O Lord, holy and true, until You judge and avenge our blood on those who dwell on the earth?"*

That is the same question that Daniel asked when he was in captivity and he saw his visions. He wanted to know how long it was going to be. This battle between good and evil has been raging for several thousand years and many people have died for the cause of good. In Hebrews 11, we can read about many great patriarchs of old who had lived and who were waiting for God's judgment. Hebrews 11: 37-38 reveals that the patriarchs waited and were martyred for the cause of Christ in many different terrible ways. They did not know Christ as yet and they cried how long, how long?

They were under the altar. In chapters 4 and 5 in the throne room, there was no mention of an altar. Where did this altar come from? Sacrifices were made on an altar. The blood of the animals which were sacrificed was poured out at the base of the altar. Therefore, where would the blood of these martyrs be? It would be at the base of the altar. They had sacrificed. They had given themselves for God's cause for good. They were given white robes. It was said to them that they should rest yet for a little season until their fellow servants also and their brethren were killed as should be fulfilled. There is more to come. The same thing was said to Daniel. Seal up the book. We cannot tell you about the rest of it yet. However, now the Revelator Jesus is opening the book and we are blessed to see the plan in its entirety. The cry of how long, how long, is going to be answered this time. Just look to the sixth seal.

When the sixth seal is opened in Revelation 6:12,

> *"Behold, there was a great earthquake; and the sun became black as sackcloth of hair, and the moon became like blood. And the stars of heaven fell to the earth, as a fig tree drops its late figs when it is shaken by a mighty wind. Then the sky receded as a scroll when it is rolled up, and every mountain and island was moved out of its place. And the kings of the earth, the great men, the rich men, the commanders, the mighty men, every slave and every free man, hid themselves in the caves and in the rocks of the mountains, and said to the mountains and rocks, 'Fall on us and hide us from the face of Him who sits on the throne and from the wrath of the Lamb! For the great day of His wrath has come, and who is able to stand?'"*

These verses by many are thought to speak of the end time judgment. I do not believe so. This sixth seal represents the culmination of the battle between good and evil. There was a war in heaven. The Bible speaks of this heavenly war a couple of times, a war between Satan and Michael, the archangel. This war was culminated by the death of Jesus Christ. Paul wrote in I Corinthians 15 that there is a victory over sin. There is a victory over death. When did this victory happen? It happened at the resurrection of Jesus Christ. It happened during that fateful time that Jesus was crucified, buried and resurrected.

In Acts 2:13, when Peter was preaching the first gospel sermon, he said the people there had witnessed that which was spoken by the prophet Joel. In Acts 2:19 Joel is quoted as saying of God,

> *"I will show wonders in heaven above and signs in the earth beneath: Blood and fire and vapor of smoke. The sun shall be turned into darkness, and the moon into blood, before the*

coming of the great and awesome day of the Lord. And it shall come to pass that whoever calls on the name of the Lord shall be saved."

Peter tells them that the day he was preaching was the fulfillment of those scriptures. It was the fulfillment of the sun being darkened and the moon being turned to blood. When we read about the crucifixion of Jesus, we are told that dead people came out of their graves and walked in the streets of Jerusalem. We read about a great earthquake. We read about the sun being darkened. We read about the moon turning to blood.

Do you remember the Roman shoulder who witnessed the death of Jesus and confessed that he was the son of God? Why would he have changed his mind after he had been responsible for killing Jesus? The Bible tells us that there were earthquakes; that the dead came out of their tombs and walked in the streets of Jerusalem. The moon turned red and that the sun went black. Darkness enveloped the earth. Some have said it was an eclipse but how can you have an eclipse of the sun and an eclipse of the moon at the same time? Nonetheless, those were events which were reported not just by the scriptures, but also by secular writers like Josephus and people who were historians who lived in that day.

The events of the sixth seal show the victory of God through Jesus Christ over the red horse in that heavenly battle. The great day of wrath has come. Satan was cast from heaven. He was put in a bottomless pit. Christ was victorious over sin and we live in that victory. In Matthew 24:34, Jesus said,

> *"Assuredly, I say to you, this generation will by no means pass away till all these things take place."*

In Luke 23:30,

> *"Then they will begin to say to the mountains, 'Fall on us!' and to the hills, 'Cover us!'"*

These words were spoken by Jesus just before the crucifixion to the people of Jerusalem about what would happen because they refused to listen to Him. Thus, we find this sixth seal showing Jesus' victory over Satan in the first century.

However, the sixth seal reveals more. In the sixth seal, John says,

> *"After these things I saw four angels standing at the four corners of the earth, holding the four winds of the earth, that the wind should not blow on the earth, on the sea, or on any tree."*

When Jesus was dying on the cross He said,

> *"My God, My God why have You forsaken me?"*

In the heavenly realm, legions of angels could come to rescue Jesus but the angels were being held back by God. They were being held back for you and for me that we might be sealed.

John saw four angels standing on the four corners of the earth holding the four winds of the earth in Revelation 7:1.

> *"Then I saw another angel ascending from the east, having the seal of the living God. And he cried with a loud voice to the four angels to whom it was granted to harm the earth and the sea, saying, 'Do not harm the earth, the sea, or the trees till we have sealed the servants of our God on their foreheads.'"*

This cataclysmic event is going to be delayed. The four angels could have come and destroyed everything at that time. Jesus said,

> *"I could call a legion of angels,"*

But He didn't.

Perhaps this angel John saw rising from the east is the resurrected Jesus. The angel cried with a loud voice to the four angels saying to hurt not the earth neither the sea nor the trees until we have sealed the servants of our God in their foreheads. The angels are held back waiting for the sealing; the sealing of those who are being saved. This is chronologically where we are today. We are in the sixth seal. Christ has ascended. The battle over evil and good has been consummated. Those who are being sealed do not have to be threatened with evil anymore, because the blood of the Lamb washes the sin away and there is no second (spiritual) death to those who live for the Lord.

The angel said not to harm them because the servants of God need to be sealed in their foreheads. What is a forehead seal? Have you ever seen anyone who had a birth mark on their face? What happens when you meet them for the first time? Your eyes are automatically attracted to the mark. You cannot help making it obvious that you are looking at the mark.

A seal in the forehead is going to be obvious. Jesus is marking your life. It will be obvious when you choose Jesus. People are going to know that there is something unique and different about you. They are going to recognize you because you are being sealed. The waiting for those four angels to destroy the earth is going on now. We are in the sealing period. We are in the sixth seal in the Book of Revelation today. We are being rescued from sure destruction by God's angels until the preaching of the gospel and the sealing is complete.

The first to be sealed are of the twelve tribes of Israel. There are 12,000 from each tribe; a total of 144,000. Now, you know as well as I do, all of the religious controversy that has arisen over the 144,000. There are even a group of people who believe that only 144,000 are going to be saved and that they have already been picked. Why anyone would want to bother with a religion like that is beyond my understanding. Again, people are caught in the trap of literal numbers. We have found no numbers so far that we believe to be literal so why this one. The number 144,000 is 12 tribes x12x1000. In the Hebrew culture, when you multiply things, the result has the properties of both the numbers. The idea conveyed by 3 x 4 we have already seen is religion. We saw this number used already in the twenty-four elders. Multiplying by 1000 would be multiplying by a very large number. As a young boy I was taught to count. I remember figuring out what to do when I ran out of fingers. First we learned the teens, and after you got to 20 you could see a pattern emerge. After I saw that, I remember going on trips in an old 1950 Plymouth Dad owned. As we went across country to my brother who went to school in Knoxville from West Tennessee where we lived, it seemed like a major migration. It took hours and hours and hours for us to get there. I would sit in the backseat of that old Plymouth and entertain myself by practicing counting. I would see how far I could count. The ultimate goal of my counting game was to make it to 1000. By that time, I understood it all and there was no limit to how far I could count. To the New Testament Hebrew mind, the idea of 1,000 is just a really big number. Sometimes they would even speak of a thousand thousands. So, 1,000 which represented a big number multiplied by 12 would imply a large number of God's followers sealed from each tribe.

In Revelation 7:9 this large counting number of God's chosen of Israel is expanded. The text says,

> *"After these things I looked, and behold, a great multitude which no one could number, of all nations, tribes, peoples, and tongues, standing before the throne and before the Lamb, clothed with white robes."*

For those people who believe that only 144,000 are being saved, I like this one better. The Revelator gives us a great multitude that no one can number. It has bothered me that there were only eight saved in the flood. I become further concerned when Jesus preaches in Mathew 7 that,

> *"Straight is the gate and narrow is the way that leads to life and few there be that find it."*

However, the Revelator reveals that few is a number larger than we might think.

The marking is to be of 144,000 of all of the tribes of Israel and a great multitude of all nations which no man could number. When Jesus gave his great commission, he instructed to go into the entire world and preach the gospel to every creature; to make disciples of all nations. We also have a great multitude, which no man can number of all nations and kindred and peoples and tongues that stood before the throne.

At the end of the sealing, at the end of the sixth seal, God will end this period of opportunity for salvation. He will bring judgment upon the world when the seven trumpets come out of this last seal.

REVELATION – CHAPTERS 8, 9, 10, AND 11

In Revelation 8:1-2 we read that when Jesus opened the seventh seal, there was silence in heaven for about the space of a half an hour. Then John saw seven angels, which stood before God and to them were given seven trumpets.

> *"Then another angel, having a golden censer, came and stood at the altar. He was given much incense that he should offer it with the prayers of all the saints upon the golden altar which was before the throne. And the smoke of the incense, with the prayers of the saints, ascended before God from the angel's hand. Then the angel took the censer, filled it with fire from the altar, and threw it to the earth. And there were noises, thunderings, lightnings, and an earthquake. So the seven angels who had the seven trumpets prepared themselves to sound."*

There was silence. It was the quiet before the storm. There was silence and the prayers of the saints were rising to heaven. God is attentive to the prayers of the saints. God is preparing to announce his judgment of the world. He is doing that because of the prayers of the saints. I remember singing a song whose final words said "Lord come quickly". I sang that song for several years without thinking about what I was saying. Then I realized how difficult it is to sing those words. Could you sing those words and it not be a lie? I have ten grandchildren in the world. I would like to see them grow up. Do you ever hope the Lord won't come right now? Revelation is telling us that there is going to come a time when we will not want to see our children grow up in this world. There is going to come a time when the world is going to grow so wicked that it was like Genesis chapter 6, when he said that the thoughts and intents of man's heart was evil continually.

It is going to be a terrible place to live because of the decisions the people have made for wrong and sin. I think we can see that beginning to happen now. We see the destruction of the family. We see our nation no longer being one nation under God and all of the embattlements that are occurring there. We see the unrest that is in the world, the Muslim world seeking to gain authority over the whole world. I can imagine the prayers of the saints saying, "God, why don't you reconcile this? Why don't you bring justice? Why don't you make it right?"

Thundering, lightning, and earthquakes followed the silence. The judgment of God was preceded by natural calamities that foreshadowed the trumpets of judgment. Just as the first four seals, the four horsemen came out just a few verses apart, the first four trumpets sounded very quickly with just a few verses between each. In chapter 8 between verse 7 and 12, we read of four of the trumpets sounding. Then, there are several verses that describe the last three.

Consider the first four trumpets, the beginning the judgments of God because of the prayers of the saints. How is that to happen? Thus far, we have been able to look at the prophecies in Revelation and talk about them in past tense. We have been able to talk about them in terms of God's creation of good and evil. We have been able to talk about them in terms of Jesus' coming. We have been able to talk about them in terms of all of those saints who died because of their love of God and their faithfulness to Him. We have been able to talk about it in terms of the sealing of those who are saved, but now, we are going to be talking about the future. How well do we see the future? Not as well as we see the past. As we talk about these trumpets, we are going to be talking about events that are yet to come and what is revealed to us is what we know. Anything beyond that is conjecture. I would warn to be careful about what we might add to this account. Rather, we listen to the things being said in the sense that they are said, and gain the lessons from them.

When the judgment of God began,

> *"The first angel sounded: And hail and fire followed, mingled with blood, and they were thrown to the earth. And a third of the trees were burned up, and all green grass was burned up."*

The first thing that happens is calamity on the earth. There are going to be phenomena that occur, either natural or unnatural which cause destruction of things on the earth.

> *"Then the second angel sounded: And something like a great mountain burning with fire was thrown into the sea, and a third of the sea became blood. And a third of the living creatures in the sea died, and a third of the ships were destroyed."*

Judgment strikes the land and the sea in quick succession. It is a picture of physical calamities that are going to occur.

> *"Then the third angel sounded: And a great star fell from heaven, burning like a torch, and it fell on a third of the rivers and on the springs of water. The name of the star is Wormwood."*

Wormwood is a Biblical metaphor for bitterness drawn from a plant by that name which was very bitter. Many men died from the water because it was made bitter. Is this the poisoning of our water supply? How does it happen? A star falls out of heaven. I do not know what John is describing. He could have been describing nuclear warheads that split into parts or it could be an asteroid. It could be any number of things. All we know is it is described as a star that comes out of the heavens and that it breaks apart and it attacks or causes trouble with a third of the rivers, the waters that we drink from, that we use from our life. Because of it, many men die

The fourth angel sounds in verse 12,

> *"And a third of the sun was struck, a third of the moon, and a third of the stars, so that a third of them were darkened. A third of the day did not shine, and likewise the night."*

Can you imagine a day that was a third shorter than it is now? Can you imagine calamities in the heavens as our sun goes out and our moon ceases to shine, the effects on the tidal waters as that moon ceases to function as it should. We see a time of great calamity occurring in quick succession, one, two, three, and four. Boom! Boom! Boom! Boom!

In verse 13,

> *"And I looked, and I heard an angel flying through the midst of heaven, saying with a loud voice, 'Woe, woe, woe to the inhabitants of the earth, because of the remaining blasts of the trumpet of the three angels who are about to sound!'"*

Here is described a division in these trumpets. The first four trumpets bring physical calamities that will cause the loss of life upon the earth. People could consider them as natural phenomenon and not consider them as having anything to do with judgment. It is bad, but we expect life to continue as usual. However, there are three woes to come out of the three trumpets that follow these four which will leave no doubt as to the judgment of God.

The first woe is revealed in chapter 9, verse 1. The fifth angel sounds and John sees a star fall from heaven onto the earth. We saw a star fall in the previous chapter that attacked the waters. We had no reason to believe that it was anything but a star or a meteor or a rocket or something that looked like a star falling. There was no pronoun reference to indicate that it was anything other than a star. However, here we have another star, a star that falls from heaven onto the earth. This star is personified by the pronoun "he". This star is perhaps an angel or some spiritual being that falls from heaven and comes to the earth.

9: 3-10

To him was given the key of the bottomless pit. He opened the bottomless pit and there arose a smoke out of the pit as the smoke of a great furnace. The sun and the air were darkened by reason of the smoke of the pit that came out. The bottomless pit is the residence of Satan since he was cast out of heaven. In Revelation 12:9 it says that the great dragon was cast out. That old serpent called the devil and Satan, which deceived the whole world, was cast out into the earth. He lost his place because of his wickedness and choice for evil. He is cast from Heaven to the earth and all of his angels were cast out with him. We discussed in the last chapter about the great battle in heaven that occurred when Jesus died upon the cross. Good and right were victorious because of the slaying of the innocent man Jesus, and through the blood of this innocent man all nations could be justified. At that point the devil suffered a great loss and lost his power. His power over man was gone because death had no victory. He was cast to the earth because he had been defeated. He was no longer a heavenly being, but bound in a bottomless pit.

However, the bottomless pit has a key and Satan is going to be released as this judgment scene begins. Out of this bottomless pit, there comes smoke, smoke which is Satan's false doctrine that deceives and hides the light. One of the frightening things in our world today is the attack on the word of God. Those who would put their trust in God are belittled and demeaned. The world practices a worship of themselves. It is seen in the way they adorn their bodies, the way they care for themselves, the way they are filled with the pleasure of sin. Not being satisfied with that, they want to attack those who believe in the truth. They send great clouds of shadow and doubt that shield the light. It is the devil's doing. The devil is attempting to remove the truth from the earth and take as many with him as he can.

Out of the smoke there came locusts which looked like scorpions upon the earth. These scorpions were given power to sting. It was commanded to them that they should not hurt the grass neither any green thing, neither any tree, but only those men which have not the seal of God in their foreheads. In the present, God sends the rain on the just and on the unjust. God does not make a distinction between blessing those who choose good and those who choose evil. God has held back the angels and reserved His judgment for a later time. However, in that later time we will see great calamities in the earth. We will see a rise and resurgence of evil within the world. We will see the truth called a lie. We will see darkness upon truth, and the light will not be able to penetrate the darkness. We will see evil people beginning to suffer because of their own wickedness. Can you imagine what it will be like when God stops treating good and evil the same way? We will be able to look and see people suffering because of the evil that is in their life.

Why do you suppose God would do that? Why do you suppose he would sting those who are wicked and spare the righteous? The purpose is to get them to change. God does not want anyone to perish. He desires all to come to repentance. Before that great judgment day, He is going to bring forth things which display the difference between good and evil in a very graphic way.

In Revelation 9:6 we read that,

> *"In those days men will seek death and will not find it; they will desire to die, and death will flee from them. The shape of the locusts was like horses prepared for battle. On their heads were crowns of something like gold, and their faces were like the faces of men. They had hair like women's hair, and their teeth were like lions' teeth. And they had breastplates like breastplates of iron, and the sound of their wings was like the sound of chariots with many horses running into battle. They had tails like scorpions, and there were stings in their tails. Their power was to hurt men five months."*

These five months are not literal anymore than any other number we have seen. It is interesting to note that the time period for locust swarming is about five months so the five months could indicate the complete life cycle of the woe. These demons that come out of the bottomless pit are compared to locusts. Locusts were greatly dreaded during the time of John because they would destroy whole crops. They would destroy your livelihood. They would produce famine in the land. They were very destructive. John describes the image of locusts which looked like horses and these locusts have stings in their tail like scorpions. They are not destroying the crops this time. They are punishing people. They are stinging them. They are not killing them. They are stinging them. They do not die. They are suffering for five months.   They have a king over them, which is the angel of the bottomless pit. These locusts are the followers of Satan and have been bound with him in the pit. They are the followers of one whose name in the Hebrew tongue is Abaddon, but in the Greek tongue has the name Apollyon.

In Revelation 9:12 we read that one woe has passed and behold there come two woes more hereafter. We have seen four trumpets that represent calamity in the physical world and a fifth trumpet sounding a battle upon the earth where the wicked are going to be oppressed. Those with seals in the forehead will not be hurt. The unmarked will experience a terrible time of suffering and of pain, but they are not going to be able to die. That is the first woe.

The next two trumpets are going to sound and produce the second and third woe. When the sixth angel sounds his trumpet, the four angels, which are bound in the great river Euphrates, are loosed and they prepare for an hour and a day and a month and a year to slay the third part of men.   The counting of an hour and a day and a month and a year is indicating that there is a very specific time that God has in mind for this next woe. He knows the day, the minute, the hour and the second that this is going to happen.   God will unleash his fury and the fury will include death, like the tenth plague on Egypt. The number of the army and the horseman was 200 thousand thousand and John heard the number of them and saw the horses in the vision. John was taken by how horrible these things were that were bringing the oppression. In Revelation 9:20 we get a hint about God's purpose in this woe. Those who were dying were the rest of the men that were not killed by these plaques yet repented not of the works of their hands. Even in judgment God is offering repentance, but the wicked will not. Even in God's patience, love and long suffering, men will continue to do evil things. Verse 21 reveals that neither they repented of their murders nor their sorceries nor their fornications nor their thefts.

In Revelation 10:1,

> "I saw still <u>another mighty angel</u> coming down from heaven, clothed with a cloud. And a rainbow was on his head; his face was like the sun, and his feet like pillars of fire. He had a little book open in his hand. And he set his right foot on the sea and his left foot on the land, and cried with a loud voice, as when a lion roars. When he cried out, <u>seven thunders</u> uttered their voices. Now when the seven thunders uttered their voices, I was about to write; but I heard a voice from heaven saying to me, 'Seal up the things which the seven thunders uttered, and do not write them.' The angel whom I saw standing on the sea and on the land raised up his hand to heaven and swore by Him who lives forever and ever, who created heaven and the things that are in it, the earth and the things that are in it, and the sea and the things that are in it, that there should be delay no longer"

There should be no more delay. In Chapter 6 when the fifth seal was opened, the saints who had been martyred stood under the altar and cried "How long, how long"? There was then the time in which the sealing of the saints occurred. Now this angel says that we are out of time. There will not be any more time. Sometimes when preachers talk about the fact that we have no promise of another invitation they remind us that we do not know the day, or the hour, or the minute when the end will come, but we do know that when it does come, there will be no more time.

There are theological ideas that propose that perhaps we will get a second chance. The scriptures do not teach that. The scriptures teach that when the day, and the hour and the time come, there will be no more delay. God has sent these signs, sought for people to repent and they have not repented. The thunders are the pronouncements of God and He sealed them up. John cannot tell what the pronouncements are but hear this; there is no more time. That is frightening. To think there is no more time. There is no more time for me to change. Whatever state I am in, that is what I am for eternity.

In Verse 7, John is told that in the days when the voice of the seventh angel shall begin to sound that the mystery of God should be finished. Near the end of the sixth angel that has sounded, the Revelator mentions the seventh angel. He says there will be time no more because when the seventh angel sounds his trumpet, it is all over.

Then something very interesting happens. It is puzzling and there have been all kind of interpretations about what it means. There is an interlude; an interlude that reveals two witnesses. All sorts of interpretations have been made of these two witnesses. I cannot say that I understand what it means, but let me explore an idea. We found that when the sixth angel sounds his trumpet that there is a tremendous amount of grief and woe that comes to those who are wicked, but they don't repent. Then, a very mighty angel comes down, puts his feet on the earth and the sea as if he is going to cover everything. He has a book in his hand, a little book, and out of it comes seven thunders, which John is not able to reveal to us and then he speaks and he says there will not be any more time because when the seventh angel sounds, it is over. What would you suppose would be the point of telling this? What should we be doing in the meantime? We should be preparing.

In Revelation 10:8, the voice which John heard is from heaven. It is not the angel talking to him but this is a voice that comes out of heaven. The voice said,

> *"Go, take the little book which is open in the hand of the angel who stands on the sea and on the earth."*

John went to the angel and asked for the little book. The angel told John to take it and eat it. He said it would make his belly bitter, but in his mouth it would be sweet as honey. How do you feel about the Lord coming right now? What is your reaction? I believe if you are like me, it would be bittersweet. It is sweet because it is what I look forward to; the spending of eternity with God. It is bitter because we realize that many are going to be lost. John is seeing the judgment of God. He takes this little book and puts it in his mouth and it is sweet. It is so wonderful to see that God is victorious. "Hallelujah Anyway." However, when it gets to his stomach, he begins to think about all of those unprepared people and what happens to them. Then John is instructed to prophecy. John, even though in exile on the isle of Patmos, is not finished. His work must continue. Here we take a break from the judgment scene and return to the time of John and his writing and teaching. The angel who came down provides an interruption in the judgment scene to reflect on the present. A flashback to John's time and the diligence needed to preach the word (be a prophet for God).

Then beginning in chapter 11;

> *"Then I was given a reed like a measuring rod. And the angel stood, saying, "Rise and measure the temple of God, the altar, and those who worship there. But leave out the court which is outside the temple, and do not measure it, for it has been given to the Gentiles. And they will tread the holy city underfoot for forty-two months."*

Some take these verses as proving that physical Israel will rebuild the temple; but where is the temple of God? It is the church, the kingdom of Christ, the saints. John is told to measure the church. That was what chapters 2 and 3 were about; measuring the church, evaluating the churches, the seven churches of Asia Minor.

God says;

> *And I will give power to my two witnesses, and they will prophesy one thousand two hundred and sixty days, clothed in sackcloth." These are the two olive trees and the two lampstands standing before the God of the earth. And if anyone wants to harm them, fire proceeds from their mouth and devours their enemies. And if anyone wants to harm them, he must be killed in this manner. These have power to shut heaven, so that no rain falls in the days of their prophecy; and they have power over waters to turn them to blood, and to strike the earth with all plagues, as often as they desire."*

This period of 42 months which is also 3 ½ years or 1,260 days is the same time spoken of in other places in Revelation. In Revelation 13:5 these numbers are used again as well as in Revelation 12:6 and Revelation 12:14. These numbers are the period of the prophecy of John and refer to the Christian Age. John has seen the judgments of God in six trumpets and two woes and John knows that the end time will come as a bittersweet message. John knows when the seventh angel blows his trumpet that it is the end and time will be no more. There will be 1,260 days or 42 months or 3-1/2 years representing the Christian Age in which John's words will be preached. Two witnesses will witness with John. The two witnesses are the same as the two olive trees and the two candlesticks. These icons are also used in the Book of Zechariah. Some have suggested that they are Elijah and Jesus while others suggest the Old Testament and the New Testament.

What is it that testifies of God in the Christian Age? God oversaw the production of the Holy Bible so that man would have the truth preserved to preach. The testimony of God in the Bible would witness to the whole world the will of God. Fire would proceed out of their mouth. On Pentecost tongues of fire sat over the apostle's heads as the Holy Spirit guided their tongue. Fire proceeded from their mouth and devoured their enemies. If any man will hurt them; he must in this manner be killed. Consider the longevity of the scriptures in light of all of the people who have tried to destroy it and yet the Bible survives.

In Hebrews 6:17-18 we read,

> *"Thus God, determining to show more abundantly to the heirs of promise the immutability of His counsel, confirmed it by an oath, that by two immutable things, in which it is impossible for God to lie, we might have strong consolation, who have fled for refuge to lay hold of the hope set before us."*

These two immutable things, these two witnesses assure us that the preaching is true.

> *"When they finish their testimony, the beast that ascends out of the bottomless pit will make war against them, overcome them, and kill them."*

What is the attitude toward the Bible today? When I was a child growing up, the Bible was the bestselling book that has ever been published. More copies of it sold than any other book published. Will that trend continue today? Will the Bible continue to be revered as God's book? When the testimony of God is complete, we will someday be guilty of killing the witness of God.

> *"And their dead bodies will lie in the street of the great city which spiritually is called Sodom and Egypt, where also our Lord was crucified. Then those from the peoples, tribes, tongues, and nations will see their dead bodies three-and-a-half days, and not allow their dead bodies to be put into graves. And those who dwell on the earth will rejoice over them, make merry, and send gifts to one another, because these two prophets tormented those who dwell on the earth."*

The wicked world will rejoice at the death of God's witness because it convicted them of their sins and held them responsible for their choice of evil. Can you imagine a time when all the Bibles are gathered and piled in the street and we are forbidden to read them, a time when the wicked shall rejoice and make merry because there is no law. John saw it happen at the end of the Christian era when Satan is released from the bottomless pit and makes war with the saints.

> *"Now after the three-and-a-half days the breath of life from God entered them, and they stood on their feet, and great fear fell on those who saw them."*

But their jubilation will be short lived for the witnesses cannot be contained and their message will again live. In Revelation 11:12 the voice from heaven comes again.

"And they heard a loud voice from heaven saying to them, 'Come up here.' And they ascended to heaven in a cloud, and their enemies saw them. In the same hour there was a great earthquake, and a tenth of the city fell. In the earthquake seven thousand people were killed, and the rest were afraid and gave glory to the God of heaven. The second woe is past. Behold, the third woe is coming quickly."

In Revelation 11:15,

"Then the seventh angel sounded: And there were loud voices in heaven, saying, "The kingdoms of this world have become the kingdoms of our Lord and of His Christ, and He shall reign forever and ever!"

After an interlude of praise by the twenty-four elders, the judgment continues in verse 19.

"Then the temple of God was opened in heaven, and the ark of His covenant was seen in His temple. And there were lightnings, noises, thunderings, an earthquake, and great hail."

So we have come to the end of Gods plan at the end of chapter 11. We have come to the end of the history of the world from a heavenly perspective. The judgment is done, the two witnesses are in heaven, the saints are raised and the third woe is executed on the wicked that would destroy the earth. The kingdom is delivered and the temple in heaven is opened. The victory over Satan and his evil is done. "Hallelujah Anyway"

REVELATION – CHAPTER 12

In Revelation chapters 4 through 11, John in a vision was lifted up in the spirit into heaven on the Lord's Day. He went through the open door of heaven. He saw the throne room of God and there he received the heavenly vision of the seven seals and the seven trumpets that came out of the seventh seal. The seven seals provided us a heavenly insight into all God's plan from the origins of good and evil to the victory of God and the judgment of the world. All of God's mystery, as Paul called it, is revealed to man.

John has recorded for us the history of the world as viewed from his position in heaven. In Chapter 12 he begins another vision which we will learn has an earthly perspective. There is no announcement that this begins a new vision, but in verse 1, we read that there appears a great wonder (sign) in heaven. A sign indicates something new was about to be revealed. Like the two dreams of Pharaoh in Genesis 41:25, Joseph interpreted, "The two dreams are one." In like manner we will recognize two major visions provided to John to reveal the mystery of God. John will see the plan of God unfold with both an earthly and a heavenly perspective.

The first two verses introduce to us a woman who is pregnant, a woman who is in the labor pains of childbirth. She is clothed with the sun. A moon is under her feet and on her head is a crown of 12 stars.

She is shown clothed with sun because of the light of truth she possessed. Paul said in Romans that the Jews had been blessed with the oracles of God. Jesus is referred to as the light of the world. In John chapter 1 we are told that the light came into the world and the darkness comprehended it not. The light would make manifest the planning of God to justify and save the lost through His son. The woman had the moon under her feet. In Bible days, time was marked by the change of the moon with a lunar calendar. This calendar marked the fullness of time for the arrival of the Messiah.

This woman surely represents Israel, the chosen nation of God revealed in the form of a woman who is in travail and bringing forth the seed of woman that is going to provide the destruction of evil and sin and Satan. From the time of Abraham God had promised that the nation of Israel, the descendents of Abraham would produce a blessing to all nations. The woman had a crown of 12 stars. This most likely represents the angels of the twelve tribes of Israel. The woman is Israel and she is giving birth to the Savior of the world, the Messiah, the Light of the world.

Another character is described in verse 3.

> *And another sign appeared in heaven: behold, a great, fiery red dragon having seven heads and ten horns, and seven diadems on his heads. His tail drew a third of the stars of heaven and threw them to the earth. And the dragon stood before the woman who was ready to give birth, to devour her Child as soon as it was born.*

The whole Bible is about Jesus. We have already noted that in Genesis 3:15, we are warned of a battle between Christ the seed of the woman and Satan.

> *"She bore a male Child who was to rule all nations with a rod of iron. And her Child was caught up to God and His throne."*

Who was caught up to God and to God's throne? Jesus. So, this is speaking of the coming, life, death, and resurrection of Jesus. The woman fled into the wilderness where God prepared a place to feed her for a thousand, two hundred and sixty days. This is the number we've discussed before that we believed referred to the Christian Age. This period of time of a thousand two hundred and three score days (42 months). It is also called a time, a time and a half-time. All of these are varied references to the same time.

Then there was war in heaven as Michael and his angels fought against the dragon and his angels. Michael through Christ was victorious and the dragon was cast out. The Revelator identifies the dragon as Satan, that old serpent. This reminds us of the temptation by Satan as a serpent in the Garden of Eden. The devil had access to heaven as we observed from the Book of Job which we discussed earlier. The devil is a created spirit of God. He is an angel. However, Satan wanted to overthrow God and he drew off a third of all of the angels. The army of Satan was a third of all of the angels, a minor portion of all of the angels of God. Not a literal number, but something less than half.

The war was between Satan and his angels and Michael, referred to as the archangel, and God and his angels. The dragon and his angels lost and they were cast out of heaven. Jesus told His disciples that He saw Satan fall like lightening from heaven. This war is also mentioned in Jude verse 9, but otherwise there is very little discussion of it in the scriptures. Apparently Satan had the ability to roam freely through heaven and earth. He was known as the accuser. He was always accusing God's people. His name even meant accuser. He was always bragging about what he could do if God didn't protect His people. He was always combating God and tempting man to sin so that God's earthly creation would fail. His warped sense of right and wrong somehow equated the failure of God's creation as a victory for himself. However, it was always God's plan that the serpent's head would be bruised as he bruises the heel of the seed of the woman. So there is a heavenly war and Satan and his angels are cast out of heaven. Satan and his angels are not allowed in heaven anymore. They are cast to the earth. These are immortal beings. They cannot be killed or destroyed and so they are cast to the earth. Satan becomes the prince of this world. Satan loses the war and is cast to the earth.

Satan is the deceiver of the whole world. He is cast out of heaven to the earth and his angels were cast out with him. While Jesus was on the earth, there was demon possession. The devil and his angels had free reign of the earth and possessed the minds and bodies of people. This deceiver of the whole world and his angels with him and was completely defeated or bound at the resurrection of Jesus.

> *"Then I heard a loud voice saying in heaven, 'Now salvation, and strength, and the kingdom of our God, and the power of His Christ have come.'"*

This is the announcement of the birth of the church, God's kingdom.

> *"For the accuser of our brethren, who accused them before our God day and night, has been cast down. And they overcame him by the blood of the Lamb and by the word of their testimony."*

We are made aware of the weapons that are successful in this war with Satan. When Jesus died on the cross, all of the great cataclysmic events that we read of; the sun being darkened, the moon turned to blood, the earthquakes and the dead walking in the street, were the ending of that war in heaven. Satan has made a terrible mistake. He has slain an innocent man, and that innocent man can now through his blood provide forgiveness of sin to all sinners. That is the death blow to Satan. Satan no longer has the power of death.

> *"O Death, where is your sting? O Hades, where is your victory?"*

Paul writes in 1 Corinthians 15.

Satan was cast down from heaven and as he continued his battle, Jesus came to where Satan was and concludes this battle by overwhelming Satan. You do not see demon possessed people anymore because Satan has been bound. He has been bound by the blood of Jesus Christ. He has been bound by the word of His testimony. Jesus, when he was tempted of the devil said;

> *"Away with you, Satan!"*

Then He quoted the scripture, the word of His testimony. We have the same ability. We overcome temptation and sin and overpower the devil by Jesus' blood and the word of His testimony.

The devil is walking the streets seeking whom he may devour, but he can only devour those who let him. We have the power to overcome Satan. He said

> *"Woe to the inhabitants of the earth and the sea! For the devil has come down to you, having great wrath, because he knows that he has a short time."*

When the dragon saw that he was cast down to the earth, what did he do? He persecuted the woman who brought forth the child, and to the woman were given two wings of a great eagle that she might fly into the wilderness into her place where she is nourished for a time and time and half a time. During the Christian age, spiritual Israel (the church) is protected and nourished.

She is helped by two wings of a great eagle. The Bible speaks of the nation of Israel being rescued on the wings of an eagle. Exodus 19:4-6 is a reference where God protects the nation of Israel with the wings of an eagle.

Jesus said of Jerusalem;

> *"O Jerusalem, Jerusalem, the one who kills the prophets and stones those who are sent to her! How often I wanted to gather your children together, as a hen gathers her chicks under her wings, but you were not willing!"*

The strength, the power and the majesty of the eagle allows Israel to escape from trouble as typified by how God protected and nourished this woman who represents physical and spiritual Israel.

The woman gives birth to a man child who rules with a rod of iron and to Him are given the kingdom and he becomes the king. Jesus defeated Satan, bound him with His blood and testimony, and ascended to Heaven to sit at the right hand of God and rule over His kingdom until all things are put under His feet. The serpent cast out of his mouth water as a flood after the woman so that he might cause her to be carried away by the flood. The devil is upset at having lost so on the earth he is creating a rampage and attacks the woman. The woman is caught up and carried away to safety, so Satan attacks the remnant. He opens his mouth as a flood of water to cause her to be carried away, but the earth opened her mouth and swallowed up the flood, which the dragon cast out of his mouth.

This water that spews out of the Devil's mouth represents the deceptive lies and evil of Satan. In Isaiah 8: 57, Isaiah describes the overwhelming temptation of the world against the nation of Israel as a sea. The lies were like a flood, a great tsunami that comes and produces tremendous damage. A symbol of what evil is like as it attempts to overwhelm us, but the earth protected the woman. It opened itself up and took in all of this water. It took in the lies. The physical things accepted the flood of lies but the spiritual did not. Galatians 5 contrasts the fruits of the spirit and the works of the flesh. The devil with the flood of the dragon cast out of his mouth was angry with the woman. He was angry with the church because he lost the battle and the war. He is bound and cast out of heaven so he makes war with the remnant of Israel. The persecution of the early church is the attack on the remnant of her seed. The remnant refers to those who keep the commandments of God and have the testimony of Jesus Christ. The remnant is the kingdom or church of Christ.

Chapter 12 is a retelling of the time when the fifth and sixth seal were opened and the sealing of the saints was occurring. The Revelator uses chronological flashback to the time of the Christian age. However the view from heaven is this time with an earthly perspective. Verse 1 of chapter 12 begins with great wonders in heaven. The wonder started in heaven but this time we are viewing the impact on earth as Christ is born, dies and is resurrected. The sign reveals the physical and spiritual

Israel giving birth to the Savior, birth to the one who would offer salvation and forgiveness of sins. Salvation has come to the earth.

> *"Then I heard a loud voice saying in heaven, 'Now salvation, and strength, and the kingdom of our God, and the power of His Christ have come.'"*

The devil had to be defeated before the church could be established. Today we fight against a defeated foe. The devil has already lost the heavenly and the earthly battle. Now the only power that he can have in our lives is what we give to him. We have weapons that overcome him. We have the blood of the Lamb, and the word of His testimony, and the absence of the fear of death. The only power Satan has left is the power of sin to separate but the blood of Jesus washes sin away. Some people will waste their lives in the seasonal pleasure of sin because they are deceived to think that this earth is all there is. These soak up Satan's flood of lies and refuse to be sealed by the Christ.

John views this sign in heaven of the Christian Age. The devil, this dragon with seven heads and seven crowns and ten horns representing his authority in earthly kingdoms is doing battle. As John's vision continues in subsequent chapters we will have revealed Satan's beasts of deception that he pours out as a flood.

REVELATION – CHAPTER 13

As we have studied together we have seen the first eleven chapters the Book of Revelation dealing with a heavenly perspective of the history of the world from the creation to the judgment portrayed in seven seals followed by seven trumpets. The visions represented the things that had been, that were, and that would come. They were the mystery that was revealed to mankind about God's plan for the world; about the sealing of those that were being saved during the period of time that we live in now and up until the judgment comes. The bottom line is that God is in charge. God is victorious. "Hallelujah Anyway" in spite of all of the things that occur as the battle between good and evil rages.

Chapter 12 begins a chronological flashback to retell God's plan from an earthly perspective. Although John sees the history of mankind again, He sees it in a much different way. It shows the mystery revealed in the nation that God has chosen to be his people and through whom the Messiah or Savior comes. That nation, Israel, is portrayed by the symbol of a pregnant woman, clothed in the sun with the moon at her feet; a woman travailing in childbirth of the Son of God. God made a promise to Abraham that through his seed all nations would be blessed. In Vacation Bible School the children sing, "Father Abraham had many sons, and many sons had father Abraham. I am one of them and so are you, so let's just praise the Lord." We are children of Abraham by the promise of the covenant that God made and that was delivered in the pregnancy of Israel. Israel was an expectant mother travailing to bring forth the Savior that would bless all nations with the promised spiritual kingdom. *Blaspheming God.* *Dragon (10 horns + 7 heads)*

In Chapter 12, Satan is cast out of heaven. He is cast to the earth. He has lost the battle of good versus evil with Michael the archangel. Satan took a third of the angels with him. Afterward, the Devil walks the earth seeking whom he may devour. He does battle against the expectant woman trying to kill the child that comes forth. The baby had to flee to Egypt to avoid death by Satan's servant. After Jesus was baptized, He was led to the wilderness by the Spirit to do battle (be tempted) with Satan.

Satan was eventually successful in destroying the child physically; but unwittingly did exactly what God had planned. Satan killed an innocent man so that the innocent blood could justify all the redeemed. We also can be justified by the blood of that innocent man. None of us are innocent, but the blood of Jesus Christ washes away sins and makes us innocent. The devil in attempting to destroy this child inadvertently destroyed his own power, the power of death. When Satan's power is bound, Satan's anger is unleashed against the seed of the woman. The seed of the woman are those who are born again through God's Son. The seed of woman is the church the spiritual kingdom of Israel. We become children of God by our faith in Jesus Christ and become Abraham's seed, recipients of the promise that was given to Abraham (Galatians 3). God protects the woman and her seed lifting them on eagle's wings and hiding them in the wilderness. In a rage, the devil pours out a great flood of water from his mouth. The flood is a flood of deceit and lies that the devil spews out of his mouth for he is the father of lies. But it is the earth (physical man) that believes the lies and opens up and swallows the water.

In Chapter 13, the Devil's flood and the tools of his lies begin to be introduced. Satan enlists help to continue to attack God's people. We are introduced to two of his beasts. John stood upon the sand of the sea and saw a beast rise up out of the sea having seven heads and ten horns and upon his horns ten crowns and upon his heads the names of blasphemy. The word blasphemy is the ridiculing or making fun of or belittling or not taking seriously the message of God. The devil tries to get us to lose respect for the message of Christ that is being delivered. He frames it as foolishness and appeals to the earthly wisdom of the masses.

Out of the sea comes the beast that blasphemes. We are all aware of this beast around us all the time. You see it when people make light of spiritual matters that are very important. Notice how much this beast looks like Satan. The heads and the horns and the crowns remind me of Satan's description in chapter 12. The beast was like a leopard. His feet were as the feet of a bear. His mouth was the mouth of a lion and the dragon gave him his power.

This beast rises up out of the sea, the sea of false doctrine. He is preaching blasphemy with human wisdom and earthly authority and power. He is supported by the kings that make laws and the intellectuals that call evil good and good evil. This beast appeals to my earthly nature, my devilish desire to be God, my sense of humanistic independence.

These words remind me of the Old Testament book of Daniel. They are repeated in Revelation 17. In the Book of Daniel these words referred to the coming kingdom of Rome. The nation of Rome was a political giant that rose up and asked people to worship the emperor Caesar instead of worshiping God. In John's time that was the beast but I suggest that there is a beast for every age. Have no doubt that there is a beast today that seeks to blaspheme the name of God and he rises up out of the lies of Satan and the sea, to teach us to belittle and deny the word of God.

The devil is a cast out angel and is created higher than men. Jesus was made like a man. The Hebrew writer said He was made a little lower than the angels. Therefore the angels are a higher creation than man. If you study angels, you will learn that they have the ability to be in multiple places at the same time. They have the ability to move very quickly from one place to another. They have the ability to appear in different forms so that you do not recognize them. So the devil has power. His power is bound by Jesus' blood and the word, but he has power that he manifests through his workings on the earth. Such things as witchcraft, sorcery, and fortune telling are earthly manifestations of the power of Satan. The witch of Endore in First Samuel was able to call Samuel back from the dead, but she was using the power of Satan. So when we read in Revelation that the power was given to this beast by Satan, understand that many things on this earth are the working of Satan and his beasts.

John saw one of the beast's heads as if it was wounded to death and the deadly wound was healed; and all the world wondered after the beast. Satan has the power to do things that appear miraculous. Even though we see something that appears miraculous, we still must test the spirits to see whether they are of God. In 1 John 4:1-2 John says to test them by asking them if they believe that Jesus is Christ, the Son of God. If they deny the Sonship of Jesus Christ, then their power is not of God. We should even test churches that don't give the glory to God. Be careful to insure you aren't deceived by churches of Satan that feast on earthly satisfaction and success. The earth will swallow that up. The warnings are clear.

> *"Because narrow is the gate and difficult is the way which leads to life, and there are few who find it."*

And they worshiped the dragon which gave power unto the beast. They worshiped the dragon, the Devil. These people worship Satan who gives the power to the beast because it satisfies their earthly desires. It was given unto him a mouth speaking great things and blasphemies and power was given unto him to continue. God allows this to go on because He wants us to choose. We can either choose this earthly power, these pleasures of sin for a season or we can choose Christ. We have to do the judging as the rider of the third horse of the apocalypse.

In Revelation 13:6,

> *"Then he opened his mouth in blasphemy against God, to blaspheme His name, His tabernacle, and those who dwell in heaven. It was granted to him to make war with the saints and to overcome them. And authority was given him over every tribe, tongue, and nation. All who dwell on the earth will worship him, whose names have not been written in the Book of Life of the Lamb slain from the foundation of the world"*

The beast blasphemed against God and made war with the saints. The beast was given power over all kindred and tongues and nations. He defeated all whose names are not written in the Book of the Lamb. Consider what people worship today when they don't worship God. They worship the beast of material power, the beast of human intellect. The beast offers those things that man can use to elevate himself.

Thirty years ago I attended a management class for my work. The class taught about identifying employee value systems; so that as a manager, one could motivate the employee to improved performance. A year ago, I took another management class. In that class I was taught that you cannot motivate people. If an employee doesn't perform, terminate him. If he does what you want, take advantage of it. The philosophy has changed. We are worshiping the beast of how to make money rather than make investments in people. The way to make big money is to take advantage of people. This beast is dangerous. All people worship him except those whose names are written in the Book of the Life of the Lamb. Christians realize that material things are not permanent and make investments in heaven rather than listen to the beast. They cling to the testimony of Christ's word and are protected by His blood.

In verse 9-10 we read,

> *"If anyone has an ear, let him hear. He who leads into captivity shall go into captivity; he who kills with the sword must be killed with the sword. Here is the patience and the faith of the saints."*

What should we do about this beast? Should we try to slay him? The answer is no. The answer is to remain faithful and be patient. Remember from the first vision, "How long oh Lord, how long?" Patiently continue to believe in those things that you put your trust in. Contend for your faith with the eternal word of God.

In Verse 11, John introduces the second beast of Satan. The first beast has great power. He is a beast that comes from the sea. He is a beast full of blasphemy and lies. He is a beast that draws away people by offering them his power. The second beast comes out of the earth. He had two long horns like a lamb. He looked like a lamb and spoke like a dragon. He speaks like the devil but he has the look of a lamb. He is a wolf in sheep's clothing. He is pretending to be Jesus so that his speech can deceive.

In verse 12,

> *"And he exercises all the authority of the first beast in his presence, and causes the earth and those who dwell in it to worship the first beast, whose deadly wound was healed."*

The first beast called people to worship the power of the dragon. The second beast causes those who listen to worship the first beast.

In verse 13-15,

> *"He performs great signs, so that he even makes fire come down from heaven on the earth in the sight of men. And he deceives those who dwell on the earth by those signs which he was granted to do in the sight of the beast, telling those who dwell on the earth to make an image to the beast who was wounded by the sword and lived. He was granted power to give breath to the image of the beast, that the image of the beast should both speak and cause as many as would not worship the image of the beast to be killed."*

Those on the earth turn to idolatry because the beast makes an idol come to life. What are the miracles that are going on in our life; miracles that would catch our eye; miracles that would make us worship things other than the one true creator and His Son Jesus Christ? What kind of idols could we raise up that would have a life of their own? Let me share one of these idols in my life. I have spent over 40 years working as an engineer. I have worked in a lot of interesting places and done a lot of interesting things. I have spent many hours in toil to make a living. At my age now, how much is all of that worth? When I was a young man I thought about how I would make my mark on the earth. How will my life be remembered? Would I be like George Washington or Abraham Lincoln? I did those things to succeed in this world. Now that I look back I realize how much of a waste all that was.

I dreamed of searching through the solar system in my lifetime and observing planets in our solar system. I was so disappointed when the government stopped chasing that dream and traded it for another dream. What are dreams made of? Unless they are based on eternal things, they just become idols. They are dead things that seem to be alive. I am still looking to explore space, but, I am not going to do it in a rocket ship. I am going to do better than that. My immortal soul will not be limited by time or space. Not only that, I will have access to the library of the Creator. I have finally discovered what is really important.

When we start complaining about something that is happening just ask the question, Will I care about this 100 years from now? If I am going to care about it a hundred years from now, then I am going to do something about it. If I am not going to care about it a hundred years from now, I am going to let it go. It is just the beast from the earth.

> *"He causes all, both small and great, rich and poor, free and slave, to receive a mark on their right hand or on their foreheads, and that no one may buy or sell except one who has the mark or the name of the beast, or the number of his name."*

Do you remember who was sealed in their foreheads in the first vision? Christians were sealed, but this beast is going to mark people in their foreheads. Do you know what he is doing? He is claiming them. He is claiming them for himself. He is marking them to confuse them with the ones who have been marked by the Savior. What is his claim? He says that no man might buy or sell except that he has the mark. He is going to hit us in our material belly button. God gave Christian's a shield of faith to turn away the sword of Satan. He gave us a breastplate of righteousness to turn away the enemy's darts. He girded our loin with truth. He covered our feet with the gospel of peace. We are protected from Satan. We are protected from his temptation. He has no power over us, but he sneaks around and shoots us in the pocketbook and kills us dead.

If you want to get between somebody and the Lord, just put money in it. We will have the ability to buy and sell only if we have his mark. We sell ourselves for the sake of money. Like the rich fool who laid up treasures on earth. They had the mark or the name of the beast or the number of his name.

"Here is wisdom. Let him who has understanding calculate the number of the beast, for it is the number of a man: His number is 666"

The number of the beast is 666. There are several ideas about what this number means. Some believe that if you use Greek letters for a person's name and take the Greek numerical value for that number and add them up, you get the numeric value of a name. The symbols that the Greeks used for counting were their letters. Unfortunately, this method of counting needs 27 letters, and there were only 24 in the Classical Greek alphabet. This meant that the Greeks had to find 3 extra symbols for the missing numbers of 6, 90 and 900. They used 3 archaic letters, which used to be in the alphabet but had been dropped as they were no longer required. They are listed below with their sounds except for the three extras where English substitutes are used.

1	2	3	4	5	6 *Added*	7	8	9
α	β	γ	δ	ε	F	ζ	η	θ
alpha	beta	gamma	delta	epsilon	digamma	zeta	eta	theta *Added*

10	20	30	40	50	60	70	80	90 *Added*
ι	κ	λ	μ	ν	ξ	ο	π	G
iota	kappa	lambda	mu	nu	xi	omicron	pi	koppa *Added*

100	200	300	400	500	600	700	800	900 *Added*
ρ	σ	τ	υ	φ	χ	ψ	ω	S
rho	sigma	tau	upsilon	phi	chi	psi	omega	sampi

The Greeks did not have a numerical zero. If you don't have any tens value, then you don't use one of the tens letters. Using letters as numbers meant a word could look like a number instead. The Greeks (and the Hebrews, who had a similar counting system) enjoyed doing this. My name is Terry. So my name in Greek would be τερρψ. Terry has a numeric value of $300 + 5 + 100 + 100 + 8 = 513$. I have been told that John F. Kennedy's name added up to 666. Hitler and Nero's name also added up to 666 by someone's counting. Although interesting, I don't believe that is what it is to be understood from this passage.

The number seven was the number for perfection. Missing perfection by one leaves you a six. Remember that this beast had horns like a lamb. Have you ever heard of a wolf in sheep's clothing? That is the picture we need to think of this beast. He is almost right. He is so close. He looks so good. Many lost will believe this beast disguised as a lamb, and mistake him for the church or the Christ. However his number is just slightly off. They are a six instead of a seven. Sometimes we refer to a beautiful woman as a 10. Now most ladies wouldn't mind being a nine but they certainly wouldn't want to be a six. This beast was short of perfection.

Hebrews did not have superlatives in their language. They could not say fine, finer and finest. Instead, they would repeat a word. They would say, "That is a pretty lady." But if she was prettier they would say, "That is a pretty, pretty lady." If she was a 10, they would say, "She is a pretty,

pretty, pretty lady. They would repeat the adjective for superlatives. That is why in the scriptures, God is referred to as "Holy, Holy, Holy, Lord God Almighty." God is not just holy. He is the holiest. Using a superlative for imperfection six is only one away from seven or perfection, but sixty-six is eleven away from seventy-seven and even more so; six hundred sixty-six is one hundred eleven away from seven hundred seventy-seven. The mark of this beast is the mark of accepting imperfection.

There was a children's movie we took the grandkids to see called "Shark Tales". It was about people making fun of a shark that was a little different. The message of the movie was that we should not be critical of others regardless of how they live. That is what we are teaching our children. However, Christianity requires that we be able to discern between good and evil just as we would black and white or light and darkness. We need to call abortion, murder and homosexuality sin. It is not okay. On every hand this beast is telling us to accept sinful things. If you miss perfection a little bit, you bear the mark of the beast. We need the perfection of Jesus and the cleansing of his sacrifice to avoid the mark of the beast. Just being a good person, living a good moral life and doing most of what is right the best I can, leaves me worshiping my own righteousness. It leaves me worshiping the beast.

Chapter 13 has introduced two beasts, one out of the sea and one out of the earth that by the flood waters of lying deceit and false teaching lead us to worship Satan the dragon and bear the mark of imperfection. Take up the armor of God and resist the devil. He will flee from you.

REVELATION – CHAPTER 14

Even though Revelation is mysterious in many ways, there are certainly things we can understand. We notice figures and images that we have seen before. Not only does this help in interpretation, but it illustrates the chronological flashbacks that connect the telling of the same story from different vantage points and with emphasis on different characters. John tells the main thread of what he saw and then flashes back to retell some event that is particularly important to the story line. The story of the two witnesses which we saw in Chapter 11 is an example of this. John's goal through Jesus Christ is to testify that God is ultimately victorious. We ought not to struggle in fear. We ought not to be overcome by evil because we know that God is going to overcome even though evil still exists in the world.

In verse 1-5 John writes,

> *"Then I looked, and behold, a Lamb standing on Mount Zion, and with Him one hundred and forty-four thousand, having His Father's name written on their foreheads. And I heard a voice from heaven, like the voice of many waters, and like the voice of loud thunder. And I heard the sound of harpists playing their harps. They sang as it were a new song before the throne, before the four living creatures, and the elders; and no one could learn that song except the hundred and forty-four thousand who were redeemed from the earth. These are the ones who were not defiled with women, for they are virgins. These are the ones who follow the Lamb wherever He goes. These were redeemed from among men, being firstfruits to God and to the Lamb. And in their mouth was found no deceit, for they are without fault before the throne of God."*

John saw a lamb. Not just lamb's horns like that deceiver Satan, but a real lamb. The lamb was introduced in chapter 4 as the Christ, the Lamb worthy to unseal the book. When John the Baptist saw Jesus, he said,

> *"Behold, The Lamb of God who takes away the sin of the world!"*

There are some who would dispute that this Lamb is Jesus because a little later in the chapter, an angel tells the Lamb what to do. Some would argue that no angel would ever tell Jesus what to do. However, soldiers in an army often speak to their captain of the things that they believe need to be done and a good captain listens to his soldiers. The symbol of the Lamb throughout the Book of Revelation refers to Jesus, the Son of God.

The Lamb was standing on Mount Zion. The city of Jerusalem was originally Mount Zion in the Promised Land. This reference would well up thoughts of an independent and glorious Jerusalem in the Jewish mind. In Hebrews chapter 12, Zion is spoken of as a place in heaven where innumerable hosts that had been delivered to heaven will come. So it has the spiritual sense of that eternal city where the ruler is Jesus.

1st Vision

Jesus is standing with the 144,000. We have already been introduced to the 144,000 in Revelation chapter 7. There the 144,000 were sealed symbolic of those who were saved out of physical Israel. They were sealed with a mark in their forehead. Here in chapter 14, the mark in the forehead is revealed to be the Father's name. The name of God is written in the forehead of the saved. Names are important. God has always been careful with names. In the Old Testament, Sarai's name was changed to Sarah by God. Abram's name was changed to Abraham by God. Jacob's name was changed to Israel by God. God was interested in what people were named because names have meaning to us. One of the names of God that I know is Christ. So it is important to be called a Christian. Paul spoke of that in 1 Corinthians Chapter 1. Paul wrote that he was amazed that the Corinthians had already begun to divide from each other and call themselves after Paul or Apollos or Peter. People were calling themselves by what things they believed and who they followed. Paul wrote,

> "Now I plead with you, brethren, by the name of our Lord Jesus Christ, that you all speak the same thing, and that there be no divisions among you."

The mark that is in their forehead is the mark of the name of God. It is not the name of some person or teaching, but of God. It is important what we are called. It makes a difference because it determines to whom we give the glory. When ladies get married, they take their husband's name as an honor to him. They bear his name. So, we who are married to Christ will wear His name and His bride, the church will wear the name of Christ.

The 144,000 that are with the Lamb are singing a new song that no one else can learn. It wasn't because the New Song was too difficult. How had these 144,000 which were redeemed from the earth learned the song? Paul writes in 1 Corinthians 3 that you have to become a spiritual person to understand spiritual things. The natural man cannot discern the things of the spirit. The 144,000 were born spiritually and can sing a spiritual song. They were not defiled with women for they were virgins. Does that imply that a man cannot have a wife? In Hebrews Chapter 13 the writer says the marriage bed is not defiled. To understand what this means, turn to 2 Corinthians 11:2 and read,

> "For I am jealous for you with godly jealousy. For I have betrothed you to one husband, that I may present you as a chaste virgin to Christ."

The church is a chaste virgin for Christ. The idea of a virgin is the idea of the spiritual purity of the bride of Christ. The bride has been washed in the blood of the Lamb and is white as snow. The church is pure. These 144,000 were the chaste virgins that were not defiled. We will be introduced later to the woman who defiles. Her name is Babylon and she is a harlot who tries to stain the purity of the seed of woman, the Bride of Christ.

The 144,000 in Revelation Chapter 7 were 12,000 from each of the 12 tribes. Ten of the tribes were scattered in the Assyrian captivity and the remnant (the remaining two) were scattered in AD70 by Rome. So the 144,000 would have been sealed or marked prior to the destruction of Israel. Then the great multitude of all nations being saved would follow in that figurative 1260 years of the Christian age. Note that this 144,000 are already in heaven. This could be those who are referred to in Hebrews chapter 11 and 12 that came out of the tribulation; that were sawn asunder, that were destroyed in all kinds of terrible ways for their love of God. Yet they did not know the revealed mystery of God in Christ. They are also the ones in Chapter 5 who were standing at the foot of the altar crying "How long, how long?" The 144,000 were those of physical Israel that kept the faith. The blood of Jesus flowed not only for those that lived after him, but for those that lived before him and his blood washed away the sins of those who in faith believed in Him prior to His crucifixion.

In verse 6, John mentions another angel. John will introduce six angels in this chapter that are involved in the harvesting of the saints as in the time of the sixth seal. Perhaps the sixth seal and six angels are meant to remind us of what we have heard. When the seventh seal was opened in Revelation chapter 8, there were seven angels that came forth that began to sound their trumpets of judgment and terrible things happened to the earth. In chapter 15 we will again observe seven angels flashed back with seven plagues of judgment. These similarities further reinforce the proposed chronological flashback of this interpretive approach.

> *"Then I saw another angel flying in the midst of heaven, having the everlasting gospel to preach to those who dwell on the earth—to every nation, tribe, tongue, and people—saying with a loud voice, 'Fear God and give glory to Him, for the hour of His judgment has come; and worship Him who made heaven and earth, the sea and springs of water.'"*

We are observing the same things that we saw before. We see those that are around the altar crying "How long, how long?" We see the angel of destruction stopped and we see the gospel preached until all of the nations are drawn unto the Lord. Here, we are seeing the same thing, just a second time and a second telling from the earthly perspective of spiritual Israel, the church, this time.

The angel has the everlasting gospel to preach to them that dwell on the earth. The word gospel here literally means good news. The everlasting good news is Christ. In John 3:16,

> *"For God so loved the world that He gave His only begotten Son, that whoever believes in Him should not perish but have everlasting life."*

This good news is going to all that dwell on the earth, to every nation and kindred and tongue. Jesus instructed,

> *"Go into all the world and preach the gospel to every creature."*

The gospel that was reserved for the 144,000 is now available to Spiritual Israel. Paul said that in his lifetime the gospel had been preached to the whole world.

In verse 8 there followed another angel saying, Babylon has fallen. The great city that made all nations drink of the wine of the wrath and her fornication. Up to now, we have not been formally introduced to this Babylon. This is the first mention of Babylon. Babylon was a sign of God's punishment. It was a symbol of everything that was opposed to the nation of Israel and its law. The word Babylon would remind Israel of God wreaking havoc upon those who were God's chosen people. In Jeremiah 51 and Isaiah 21, Babylon is spoken of as fallen. This would symbolically mean freedom from slavery and bondage. The second angel announces the victory of God's people. The first angel says preach the everlasting gospel. The second angel says the things that oppress you are not going to be in the way anymore. You are no longer going to be a slave. You are going to be free. In Galatians 3:26-28, Paul wrote,

> *"For you are all sons of God through faith in Christ Jesus. For as many of you as were baptized into Christ have put on Christ. There is neither Jew nor Greek, there is neither slave nor free, there is neither male nor female; for you are all one in Christ Jesus."*

Babylon has fallen because of the everlasting gospel that is being preached

In Verse 9-11 the third angel followed saying with a loud voice,

> *"Then a third angel followed them, saying with a loud voice, 'If anyone worships the beast and his image, and receives his mark on his forehead or on his hand, he himself shall also drink of the wine of the wrath of God, which is poured out full strength into the cup of His indignation. He shall be tormented with fire and brimstone in the presence of the holy angels and in the presence of the Lamb.' And the smoke of their torment ascends forever and ever; and they have no rest day or night, who worship the beast and his image, and whoever receives the mark of his name."*

The third angel announces the destruction of those who have the mark of the beast in their forehead or their hand. Why is it forehead and hand? It is because it is both thoughts and deeds. The mark in the forehead was visible that indicated your allegiance and the mark in the hand was the ability to buy, sell or trade. And the number of the beast was 666. The third angel announces the destination of those who are wicked. The angel pronounces everlasting fire, the tormenting of hell to this destruction.

In verse 12-13,

> *"Here is the patience of the saints; here are those who keep the commandments of God and the faith of Jesus. Then I heard a voice from heaven saying to me, 'Write: Blessed are the*

dead who die in the Lord from now on'. 'Yes,' says the Spirit' that they may rest from their labors, and their works follow them.'"

This verse is often used at a funeral. A verse that proclaims that people who serve the Lord will rest from their labors and they are blessed even though they are dead because they have joined the 144,000. There are two things that prove the patience of the saints. Number one, they keep the commandments and number two they keep their faith. It is the belief and obedience which distinguishes those that are being saved from those that are being lost. We are marked by our continued belief and obedience.

In verse 14-16,

> *"Then I looked, and behold, a white cloud, and on the cloud sat One like the Son of Man, having on His head a golden crown, and in His hand a sharp sickle. And another angel came out of the temple, crying with a loud voice to Him who sat on the cloud, 'Thrust in Your sickle and reap, for the time has come for You to reap, for the harvest of the earth is ripe.' So He who sat on the cloud thrust in His sickle on the earth, and the earth was reaped."*

This angel (angel number 4) tells the Son of Man to reap the earth for the harvest is ripe. [wheat] The Greek word for ripe used here is the word for ripe wheat. When I first started gardening one of the things that had to be learned was how to tell when the harvest was ready to pick. A tomato is not too difficult, it turns bright red. But with corn the fruit is covered up so you wait till the silk turns brown. My Dad told me to press on the ear of corn with your finger and when it is full and tender it is ready to pull. I didn't know how until someone told me. Wheat, I understand turns a lighter color when it is ripe. This Greek word for ripe wheat means to dry up or to whither. This is significant because Jesus gave a parable in Mathew 13 about the wheat and the tares. He instructed the servants in that parable to let them grow together until time for the harvest. The wheat is going to turn golden brown and be ready to reap with the sickle because it is ripe. Wheat is a symbol of righteousness, of righteous men. The parable of the tares reminds us that judgment is taking place as this sickle is reaping from the field the church.

In verse 17, another angel (number 5) came out of the temple, which is in heaven. The angel had a sharp sickle and another angel (number 6) came out from the altar. This angel had power over fire and cried with a loud cry to him that had the sharp sickle to gather in the clusters of the vine of the earth for they are fully ripe. The wheat was ripe. Now the grapes are ripe, but we have a different Greek word. The Greek word for the wheat being ripe was withered or dried up. The word ripe for the grapes is to flourish and come to maturity. Remember when Abraham was told he must wait for the Promised Land it was because God would wait until the iniquity of the Amorites was full. A distinction is made between the kinds of crops and compares the wheat to the righteous and the grapes to the wicked. The wheat is cut and gathered into the barn when it is finished, but the grapes are put in the wine press and tortured when they are full. The angel thrust in his sickle into the earth and gathered the vine of the earth and cast it into the great wine press of the wrath of God. The winepress was trodden out of the city and blood came out of the winepress even under the horse's bridles by the space of one thousand six hundred furlongs. That is about 200 miles of blood that came out of the winepress of God's judgment. Did you notice that the Son of Man gathers the wheat and puts it in His barns, but the angel of God reaps with a sharp sickle the grapes and puts them in the winepress of the wrath of God? When Christ comes again with His mighty angels He will reap the righteous but the angels will execute His wrath on those who know not God and who obey not the gospel.

REVELATION - CHAPTER 15

Revelation chapter 15 contains only 8 verses. This chapter is the wrath of God on the wicked in this second viewing of the history of the world in the battle between good and evil. This chapter reveals again the victory that God will have so, "Hallelujah Anyway".

In Chapter 12, two characters are introduced. One is a woman with child. She is clothed with the sun; the moon is at her feet and she has twelve stars around her head. She is the picture of God's chosen people, physical Israel and spiritual Israel, the church. God's people are the children of Abraham by physical birth or by adoption (spiritual birth). Israel is pictured in labor to give birth to the promised seed. The second character is Satan pictured in red. He is portrayed as a dragon having seven heads with crowns on each head. There is a continuing battle between Israel and the dragon.

There is a war in heaven and a third of the angels side with Satan. Michael, the archangel, is commander of God's army and is victorious. I believe that a part of this battle that raged in heaven involved Jesus coming to the earth and becoming victorious over Satan. Satan kills Jesus Christ, an innocent lamb. Satan's power is destroyed when Jesus is brought forth from the tomb and death has no power over him. He no longer has the strength to deceive and is cast from heaven to the earth along with his angels. The devil is bound by the blood and the word but continues to try to torture the seed of Israel. The Lord gives wings to spiritual Israel that allows her to fly into the wilderness and there be safe from Satan's temptations. The Bible teaches that there is no temptation given greater than we can bear. Satan has no power over us. The power of sin and death has been removed by the blood of Jesus Christ. He can have no power over us that we do not give to him.

In chapter 13 two beasts that Satan brings forth to help him are described. One comes from the sea and the other comes from the earth. Coming from the sea signifies coming from the multitudes and teaching false doctrine that is opposed to Christ. Coming from the earth signifies being deceived by materialism and humanism. The beast from the earth teaches you to worship the first beast and draws you away from the need of God. These beasts are the world of the Christian age that we live in today. Chapter 14 continues the discussion of the same age through the appearance of six angels but with emphasis on the preaching of Jesus and the harvest of souls.

In chapter 15 John writes,

> *"Then I saw another sign in heaven, great and marvelous: seven angels having the seven last plagues, for in them the wrath of God is complete."*

John reports this as great and marvelous. When we see good overcome evil then that is a wonderful thing. When we see the powers of right overcome wrong and the glory of light overcome darkness it is a marvelous thing. We rejoice in the victory that is Christ Jesus. These seven angels have the seven last plagues, for in them is filled up the wrath of God. These remind me of the trumpets of judgment vision of chapter 5 through 11. In that vision the seventh seal was opened and seven trumpets came out. These seven trumpets brought forth the judgment of God.

In Chapter 15, we see the repeat of that previous vision. These angels have bowls that are filled up with the wrath of God. Anger or wrath is not a sin. The scriptures teach us to be angry and sin not. There are examples in the scripture where Jesus was angry, but it was a righteous anger, a righteous indignation. It was not selfish or self-centered or vengeful. It was an attack against things that were evil and things that were wicked.

John writes,

> "And I saw something like a sea of glass mingled with fire, and those who have the victory over the beast, over his image and over his mark and over the number of his name, standing on the sea of glass, having harps of God."

This is the second time we have seen the sea of glass. The first time was in Chapter 4 where it is in front of the throne of God and was clear as crystal. It was calm. There was nothing happening on the sea. In this vision however, the sea of glass at the time of the wrath of God is mingled with fire. Standing on it are those who had gotten victory over the beast, over his image, and over his mark. Jesus walked on water and so will we who are victorious over the beast. How do we get victory over the beast? What has the power to destroy the beast? The power is the in the blood of Jesus. That power was given to these and they have victory over the beast and over his image.

The second beast made an idol that was to be worshiped by men. Idol worship may sound foreign to us today but there are many idols in our world today. Anything we chose to worship and put before God becomes our idol. My job can become an idol. Sports can become an idol. Fishing can become an idol. Golf can become an idol. The idols that the second beast builds are those things of the earth that might cause us to worship them rather than God. But those standing on the sea have overcome his image and they have overcome his mark. They stand on the sea of glass and they hold the harps that God provides and they sing the song of Moses. In the previous chapter, there were 144,000 delivered up to heaven. These 144,000 we found in the first vision were representative of those of Israel who remain faithful to God throughout the history of the physical Israelite nation. In addition though, we saw a multitude of people from other nations and other places that were marked in the forehead after that. The 144,000 are already in the throne room and now through the sea of glass is coming all of these who have overcome the dragon on the earth. These are the redeemed. These are those who have been washed by the blood of the Lamb. It is you and me. It's the church, the bride of Christ being harvested, being resurrected.

Why is the sea of glass mingled with fire? What does that mean? Fire is cleansing. Fire is purifying. In 1 Corinthians 3:13-15 we are described as being saved as though through fire. Our unrighteous works covered by the blood of Jesus cannot enter heaven so they are purged by the fire of the sea of glass.

> *"The fire will test each one's work of what sort it is and if anyone's work which he had built on endures, it will receive a reward, but if anyone's work is burned, he will suffer loss, but he himself will be saved yet so as through fire."*

When I moved to Tennessee I wanted to own some land and the Lord blessed me and allowed me to buy a little piece of land and then grow it a little at a time until eventually I surrounded myself with a large tract of land. However, a few years ago, God revealed to me that the land does not belong to me. I have the deed to it but I cannot take it with me. It is going to stay here when I leave this earth. I heard a story about a man who wanted to take his gold to heaven. He loaded up the pockets of the suit he was to be buried in with gold. He lined his casket with gold. When he came into heaven Peter asked him why he chose to bring pavement with him. The things that we sometimes consider worth so much are just going to be burned up. We are going to get no reward for the things that we have accumulated that are not heavenly in nature.

They were singing the song of Moses. In the previous chapters the 144,000 were singing a new song. The new song is mentioned several times in Psalms. The Hebrews' new song is going to be sung in heaven and it is going to be a song that no one can learn except those who are washed by the blood of the Lamb. Here the hosts that are coming through the sea of glass are singing too. They are singing the song of Moses and the song of the Lamb. The song of Moses is a song of deliverance. It is a song that God told Moses to write. It is recorded in Deuteronomy, but what is the song of the Lamb? The words to the song of the Lamb are here in chapter 15.

> *Great and marvelous are Your works, Lord God Almighty! Just and true are Your ways, O King of the saints! Who shall not fear You, O Lord, and glorify Your name? For You alone are holy. For all nations shall come and worship before You, for Your judgments have been manifested."*

In verse 5-6 John continues,

> *"After these things I looked, and behold, the temple of the tabernacle of the testimony in heaven was opened. And out of the temple came the seven angels having the seven plagues, clothed in pure bright linen, and having their chests girded with golden bands."*

Some people expect another temple to be built on earth but the only new temple is to be in heaven. I am convinced from the scriptures that God never intended man to build a temple. The prophecy that God gave to David was misinterpreted by David and Solomon. God told David that his son would build the temple. However the son of David referred to Jesus of the lineage of David. Jesus said every stone in the physical temple of His day would be torn down and the temple, His physical body, would be raised up in three days. The temple of God is in heaven. God would not dwell in a temple made with hands. The only temple on this earth is the temple of our bodies (1 Corinthians 6:19) and that is where God dwells on the earth. God builds us and he chooses to dwell in us if we allow Him. Those who look for the rebuilding of a physical temple have missed the spiritual lesson of Jesus.

No man was able to enter into the temple until the seven plagues of the seven angels were fulfilled. This time is referred to as a time of silence in the previous vision, a time in which no one could enter into the temple. We continue to see the parallels between the first vision and the second vision, the sevens, the battle n between good and evil, the seven plagues, the seven last plagues of the wrath of God and so forth.

I pray that Revelation is coming alive for you. I hope that you can see in this book that God intended for us to know that He will be victorious over evil and the words "Hallelujah Anyway, Hallelujah Anyway" will ring out.

REVELATION – CHAPTER 16

> *"Then I heard a loud voice from the temple saying to the seven angels, 'Go and pour out the bowls of the wrath of God on the earth.'"*

This chapter describes God's judgments and they are righteous. It is right to punish wrong. It is right to bless that which is good. That is justice and that is righteousness and that is what God delivers. These bowls represent the wrath of God against those who would try to destroy those things that are good and those things that are right.

In verse 2-4,

> *"So the first went and poured out his bowl upon the earth, and a foul and loathsome sore came upon the men who had the mark of the beast and those who worshiped his image. Then the second angel poured out his bowl on the sea, and it became blood as of a dead man; and every living creature in the sea died. Then the third angel poured out his bowl on the rivers and springs of water, and they became blood."*

These first three angels pour out God's punishment upon the earth and upon those that have the mark of the beast and those that worship the image.

This beast came from the sea and put a mark on people so they could trade, buy and sell and do commerce and the second beast would cause them to worship the first beast and material things. These punishments are poured out only to those who are evil. This pouring out is affecting those people who have the mark of the beast and who have worshiped his image.

The first bowl is poured upon the earth. This could mean the literal earth or those things of the earth. It could mean physical destruction and cataclysmic things that happen to the earth. In Mathew 25, when Jesus is questioned about what the end-time would be like, He talked about things that were going to happen before the destruction of Jerusalem as well as things that were going to happen before the end of the earth. As he spoke about the destruction of Jerusalem, He described earthquakes and great calamities on the earth. It is not unlike God to do that again. In the Old Testament when it refers to the day of the Lord, there were great cataclysmic events. These events could also precede the final judgment of God represented in this pouring out.

The second bowl is poured out on the sea. The sea becomes blood. Every living soul died in the sea. The word soul is from an Old Testament word for creature or being. Every creature in the sea died when the water became blood. Can you imagine how terrible that would be? That happened in a smaller way when the Nile River became blood during Moses' plague.

The third angel poured out his bowl on the rivers and waters and they became blood. All of the water on the earth became blood. Then there is an interlude in which the righteousness of these acts is defended. They are righteous because the blood they have to drink is blood that they have shed. The blood-thirsty people who kill and destroy and maim because of their own selfish desires are now rewarded with the same.

In verse 8,

> *"Then the fourth angel poured out his bowl on the sun, and power was given to him to scorch men with fire. And men were scorched with great heat, and they blasphemed the name of God who has power over these plagues."*

They repented not and would not give glory to God. There is not only earthly calamity, but heavenly calamity as well. This heavenly calamity involves the sun. The sun gets extremely hot. In the first vision we saw that there was a cutting back of the sun. Is that a conflict in the two visions? Science has studied stars and has modeled the lifetime of a star like our sun. Scientists believe that the sun is powered by nuclear fusion. The fusion is produced by the compression of gases into a very tight mass until the atomic collisions produce a nuclear fire. After the nuclear fire begins, it propagates, and becomes very intense and hot. Then over a period of time, it runs out of fuel and shrinks. As it shrinks it compresses more and more such that before it goes out it gets hotter. Thus, before the sun is completely consumed and it goes out there would be a period of time when the heat of the sun would increase.

The current talk is about global warming. There is very little definitive proof that we are in a period of global warming, but if we were, it would have very destructive effects upon the earth. The melting ice caps would cause floods in coastal areas, vegetation would be scorched and famines would follow. Many lives would be threatened and destroyed. Men were scorched with great heat and they blamed God. They blasphemed Him who had the power over these plagues and they repented not. It appears that during this period of time that people will have the opportunity to repent and say that God is right and these punishments are righteous. But the people do not repent. We will reach a time where people will not believe. People will not turn to God and God will bring righteous judgment upon the wicked.

In verse 10, the fifth angel pours out his bowl upon the seat of the beast and his kingdom was full of darkness. This seat of the beast in the New King James Version is called the throne of the beast. In the Book of Revelation, the only other throne that is mentioned is in heaven. However, this throne is an earthly throne. It could indicate a merging of all nations such that there is one seat of power and it is the seat of the beast. That is, Satan has gained power over the men that are left on the earth and they have been deceived and gnawed their tongues from the pain. Can you imagine chewing your tongue because you were in such pain? They blasphemed the God of heaven because of their pains and their sores and they repented not of their deeds.

In verse 12, the sixth angel poured out his bowl upon the great river Euphrates and the water thereof was dried up so the way of the kings might be prepared. The river Euphrates flowed out of the Garden of Eden. A great city called Babylon was built on the river. In the Book of Daniel when the seventy years of punishment had ended for God's people a king by the name of Belshazzar saw a hand that wrote on the wall the words MENE, MENE, TEKEL UPHARSIN (You have been weighed in the balances and found wanting). That very night the nation of Babylon was overthrown. The river Euphrates ran through the city of Babylon. There were gates at each end of the city where the river flowed through so that marauding armies could not come in. The Persian army built a dam above the river and diverted the waters so they could march their army in the dry canal underneath the gates of the city. Because the Babylonians were partying, the Persian army would then take the city without any of the Babylonians realizing what happened. The river Euphrates represented a source of fresh water and a barrier to enemy armies. The kings of the east were the people who oppressed physical Israel. They are the people whom God used to punish His people when they were evil. God is going to dry up the things that protect people from marauding armies.

In verse 13, John saw three unclean spirits like frogs come out of the mouth of the dragon, out of the mouth of the beast, out of the mouth of the false prophet for they are the spirits of devils working miracles and going forth unto the kings of the earth to gather them to the battle of that great day of God Almighty. People in this verse are so prideful, so full of their own power that the devil sends out his lies to appeal to them to let them believe they are as powerful as God. That is what the devil believes about himself and that is what he wants us to believe. We can make our own choices and our own decisions. We do not have to ask God. We can use logic and reasoning and we can think our way through this thing and we can build philosophical ideas that would prevent the need to ever study God's word. We certainly see this happening today. God is allowing these people with their pride to even *contemplate* fighting God. The devil is prodding man along, cheerleading for them and encouraging them in this folly. Satan is working miracles and deceiving them about the things that they are able to do. Imagine when all small nations with malicious dictators achieve nuclear capability. We see these things coming and some day there will be a battle for superiority.

Jesus says,

> *"Behold, I am coming as a thief. Blessed is he who watches, and keeps his garments, lest he walk naked and they see his shame."*

Here is another blessed in the Book of Revelation. It is a reaction to the judgments that are pouring out. What are Christians supposed to do about all of this? We can't change it. We can only watch and wait for the coming of Christ when He will be victorious so "Hallelujah Anyway."

They gathered them all together in a place called Armageddon, in the Hebrew tongue, which literally means the valley of Megiddo. This is a valley in the northeast part of Israel that was a pass through the mountains. Many years ago when we were in Colorado Springs, we lived at the foot of mountains that rise up to the west of Colorado Springs. Those mountains are very massive. To cross those mountains is terribly difficult. Many of them are snow capped and many have peaks above the tree line. People looked for a place to go through the mountains without climbing them. They looked for a mountain pass. Just to the west Colorado Springs is a mountain pass called Ute Pass. It is the reason for the city of Colorado Springs. As people migrated west they were drawn to this pass in the mountains where they could cross. It was also true in the valley of Megiddo. As a result many times armies would secure the tops of these mountains so that when an enemy army marched through the valley, they would swoop down and destroy them. Megiddo was an area where there had been a lot of battles. John uses this place as a symbol that people of his day would understand to say there is going to be a tremendous battle, a battle like those of Armageddon. This great battle is the last attempt of Satan and his followers to overthrow God. Just as there was a war in heaven when the devil was cast out, so also there will be a war on the earth which will result in the final destruction of the devil.

> *"Then the seventh angel poured out his bowl into the air, and a loud voice came out of the temple of heaven, from the throne, saying, 'It is done!' And there were noises and thunderings and lightnings; and there was a great earthquake, such a mighty and great earthquake as had not occurred since men were on the earth. Now the great city was divided into three parts, and the cities of the nations fell. And great Babylon was remembered before God, to give her the cup of the wine of the fierceness of His wrath. Then every island fled away, and the mountains were not found. And great hail from heaven fell upon men, each hailstone about the weight of a talent. Men blasphemed God because of the plague of the hail, since that plague was exceedingly great."*

God has all those things in his charge. At the end of the battle, there is a great earthquake and we observe 100 pound hail stones falling from heaven on the wicked.

Chapter 16 says things are done. Things are finished. So what is the rest of Revelation about? There are 22 chapters. What about the last six chapters? Again, the author will reflect upon some of the things that have already been discussed. As we had a second look at this vision from Chapter 12 through 16, we are going to get another look at what happened to Babylon, another look at what becomes of the Devil and the judgment day and the delivery of the new heaven and the new earth.

REVELATION - CHAPTER 17

In chapter 17, we are introduced to the third beast of Satan. This beast was mentioned in the previous chapter where its destruction was described. John began this chapter when one of the seven angels who had the seven bowels talked with him saying,

> *"Come, I will show you the judgment of the great harlot who sits on many waters, with whom the kings of the earth committed fornication, and the inhabitants of the earth were made drunk with the wine of her fornication."*

The angel carried John away in the spirit into the wilderness where he saw a woman sitting upon a red beast full of names of blasphemy. The beast had seven heads and ten horns. The woman was dressed in purple and scarlet color and wore gold and precious stones and pearls. She had a golden cup in her hand that was filled with the filthiness of her fornication. On her forehead was written, "Mystery, Babylon the great." This third beast was the mother of harlots and the abominations of the earth. John saw the woman become drunk with the blood of the saints and with the blood of the martyrs of Jesus.

We have seen a woman in Chapter 12 already. This is the second woman that we have seen. These two women are contrasted. The one woman is a righteous woman, a woman who was chosen to be God's chosen people, a woman who was elected by God. This second woman came from Satan. She was riding on a beast whose description is the same as the first beast. We have noted that the first beast represented the pride of life. This woman riding upon the beast is full of blasphemy. The first beast, as you recall, was teaching blasphemy. Blasphemy is belittling, ridiculing, making light of God and teaching that it does not matter what God commands. This woman called Babylon is full of blasphemy and she is full of fornication. She is drunk with the wine of fornication and is called a harlot. Babylon is selling the pleasures of sin for a season. She sits upon the beast which comes out of the sea of people, out of the pride of life and is saying to seek the good life. She teaches that one should live life with gusto and get everything you can now. Her teaching is completely foreign to the will of God. Babylon is arrayed in purple and scarlet and dressed with gold and precious stones and pearls which she has received from the second beast, which came from the earth. She looks prosperous and wealthy. She is mysterious and alluring.

Her name is Babylon the great. This name would remind the Jews of a city and a nation that God used to overthrew and enslave them. In the Book of Genesis, it tells of a man that established a city and built a tower to reach into heaven. That tower became known as the tower of Babel. Babylon has as its root the word Babel. To babble is to utter words which are empty. That city was making a name for itself, making a tower to reach heaven so they would be like God. They thought they could do it because the devil planted it in their mind. The devil will plant in your mind that you can even do battle with God for what you believe is right. That is what the devil did and the devil wants to teach you to do the same. The devil wants you to doubt God, to call evil good and good evil. The devil's words are Babel. That is Babylon.

That great harlot will sell you things that are not real, pleasures for a season. Those of you who are married know that you cannot buy the relationship that exists between a husband and a wife. It is not for sale. God instills within us that relationship, and it represents Christ and the church. Paul explained that when you join yourself to a harlot, you destroy God's temple. Babylon is telling lies and deceiving people because Satan wants them to be destroyed.

John said, "I saw the woman, drunk with the blood of the saints and with the blood of the martyrs of Jesus." The ones who kill the saints and martyrs are those who are falling for her lies. To believe the lies of Satan, you have to destroy what is right. People who sin do not want to sin by themselves. They are uncomfortable with the light of truth and seek to destroy it. They want to destroy any who would not believe as they do.

John says that when he saw her he wondered with great admiration. When a human looks upon Babylon, it looks good. John wondered with great admiration. He admired her. He was not repelled by her evil. He was not repelled by the blood that she carried in the cup. He was attracted. The angel said unto John,

> *"Why did you marvel? I will tell you the mystery of the woman and of the beast that carries her, which has the seven heads and the ten horns. The beast that you saw was, and is not, and will ascend out of the bottomless pit and go to perdition."*

John is told that this beast and this woman are going into destruction. Later in Revelation, we will see the judgment of God at the great white throne. God will judge those who come from the bottomless pit. Satan and a third of the angels who were wicked are reserved there for the judgment. They are going to be cast into that lake which burns with fire where there is weeping and gnashing of teeth separated for eternity from the presence of God.

The beast and the woman were and are not. They appear to be real, but they are not. In 2 Corinthians 4, Paul states that the things that are eternal are real. The other things that we see are temporary. Is the building you are in real? Most of us would say, yes it is real. I can touch it. I can see it. I can handle it. But Paul says if you see it, it is temporary. Look ahead 100 years from now. Will this building still be here? It was and it is not. It is not real. It is not eternal. Eternal things of God will be here 100 years from now. What man has made is most likely not going to be here 100 years from now. The angel says you see it, but it isn't real. You see it, but it will not last. You see it, but it is just a mirage.

Several years ago in a Toastmaster's speech contest, I delivered a speech about the pursuit of happiness. The speech was introduced with the opening of our Bill of Rights that said all men have certain unalienable rights and that among these are life, liberty and the pursuit of happiness. This indicates our forefathers understood that happiness is not an end in itself. The speech continued with an illustration from my childhood. As a boy, I saw a picture in a magazine of a miniature electronic tape recorder. It was a battery powered transistorized tape recorder. It was a small reel to reel tape recorder. It had tiny little reels with magnetic tape to record. I thought how wonderful it would be to have one and how many ways I could use it. I wanted to order that tape recorder more than anything in my life. It cost $79. That was like a million dollars to me since I only worked as a paper boy. I had a piggy bank that I kept my change in that that I earned from the paper route. Every week I would take the piggy bank out, pull the cork out of the bottom, fish all the money out and count it. I waited months and months and saved my money and finally, I had $79. Happily, I ordered the tape recorder. I was so excited. Every day I would go to the mail box. I worried the mailman to death. It took two or three weeks for the recorder to come. When it finally arrived, I was so excited. I put the batteries in. I put the tape reels on, threaded the tape through the record heads and started it up. I said, "Hello, hello, testing 1, 2, 3." I rewound it and it repeated, "Hello, hello, testing 1, 2, 3." I put the recorder on the shelf and that was the end of it. It was, but it is not. Have you ever had anything that disappointed you? Something that you thought that you just had to have and when you got it, it was empty? These experiences remind us that we need to lay up treasures in heaven where they will last. The promises of Satan are temporary. They are mirages. They are for a season. They are, but they are not.

In verses 8-14 John relates;

> *"And those who dwell on the earth will marvel, whose names are not written in the Book of Life from the foundation of the world, when they see the beast that was, and is not, and yet is. Here is the mind which has wisdom: The seven heads are seven mountains on which the woman sits. There are also seven kings. Five have fallen, one is, and the other has not yet come. And when he comes, he must continue a short time. The beast that was, and is not, is himself also the eighth, and is of the seven, and is going to perdition. The ten horns which you saw are ten kings who have received no kingdom as yet, but they receive authority for one hour as kings with the beast. These are of one mind, and they will give their power and authority to the beast. These will make war with the Lamb, and the Lamb will overcome them, for He is Lord of lords and King of kings; and those who are with Him are called, chosen, and faithful."*

This is one of the places where the historical view of the Book of Revelation arises. This view sees these seven mountains and remembers that Rome was built on seven mountains. It very well could have been an idea for that time, but does that have application for us today? Remember that seven is not necessarily a counting number but represents the idea of completeness while mountains represented authority. The vision could represent those who have complete authority, like kings and rulers. There are ten kings which have received no kingdom as of yet but received power as kings one hour with the beast. This is not a literal hour but a short period of time. In those short periods of time people will sign up with the beast because they desire worldly things.

We have seen earlier in the Book of Revelation where God used the earth to swallow up those things that would destroy the church. In light of this, these seven mountains, these seven kings and then the ten kings, which received no kingdom yet represent many generations who are going to follow the rise and fall of kings for the lure of material things which Satan offers to them. The Lamb is going to overcome them. There are going to be people rise up with false ideas planted by Satan. They will extract their power from the devil. The Lamb is the King of Kings. He is the Lord of Lords. If I put my trust in Him, though I was to die, yet shall I live. They that are with Him are called chosen and faithful. The angel then reveals that the waters on which the harlot sat were peoples and multitudes and nations and tongues. We have already talked about the sea being a sea of people. The kingdoms of these rulers spring up from the sea of people that are lost and deceived by the lies of Satan. The sea in the Book of Isaiah represented the hoards of barbarians that would come in and overthrow Israel.

> *And the ten horns which you saw on the beast, these will hate the harlot, make her desolate and naked, eat her flesh and burn her with fire.*

There is no honor among thieves. Those people are going to make allegiance with Satan and then they are going to fight one another. That is the lot of the world to make her desolate and naked and eat her flesh and burn her with fire. She is Babylon. Even today Babylon is in a war torn country with unrest politically and morally. The Middle East has been full of unrest as long as I can remember.

> *"For God has put it into their hearts to fulfill His purpose, to be of one mind, and to give their kingdom to the beast, until the words of God are fulfilled."*

We can find many contrasts in the visions of these two women. One was clothed with the sun and had the moon as her feet and other woman rode upon the second beast. The woman, who is godly, is clothed with the things of God. The woman who is earthy is clothed with things that women of the Lord are told to avoid. One was travailing in birth and the other one was travailing in death. The offspring of one is the Messiah. The offspring of the other is harlots and abominations. One of them had to flee to the wilderness. When John goes to see the harlot riding upon the first beast, it is in the wilderness. You do not see any difference in English, but in the Greek, there is a difference. Both of the words translated wilderness are the same Greek word but the reference in chapter 12 is preceded with an article. When an article is in front of a noun in Greek it means a very specific instance of the noun. When the woman was caught up into the wilderness God had prepared a specific place for her. The harlot's wilderness has no article. She was just in the wilderness, a place where it was wild, and a place where it was barbaric. Babylon is the entire figure of worldliness.

This is the greatest power the devil has against the children of God. She is the lust of the flesh riding on the pride of life.

Now we have the three beasts. The beast which came from the sea represents the pride of life. The beast which came from the earth represents the lust of the eyes and the harlot Babylon that rode upon the first beast represents the lust of the flesh. Those are the earthly tools of the dragon Satan.

REVELATION - CHAPTER 18

Babylon is referenced many times in Old Testament prophecies. Babylon was the capital city of the Babylonian Empire. It was one of the first great world empires which was very successful and used by God to punish the Israelite nation because of their wickedness. The Children of Israel were carried away for seventy years into captivity during the time of Daniel and Ezekiel and Isaiah and Jeremiah. These prophets in the Old Testament wrote about the wickedness of the city of Babylon, yet God used this wicked nation to punish His own people who were disobedient to him. However, the promise was made to the prophets that God would someday bring those nations into judgment as well. In the Book of Daniel the city of Babylon was overthrown and the Medo-Persian Empire became dominant. Their empire was a greater kingdom than Babylon had been. Their empire was overthrown by Alexander the Great and became the Greek Empire. The Greeks were eventually overthrown by the Roman Empire which was in existence during the time that John wrote Revelation.

Babylon was noted as being on seven hills and since Rome was set on seven hills, some have thought that this Babylon was figurative of Rome and the wickedness of Rome. Rome had become very wicked. They oppressed Christians. They practiced homosexuality. There were large numbers of pedophiles. It was a very wicked time and the church opposed the wickedness. However, this vision also has modern application because these two beasts represent the pride of life and the lust of the eye. With these two together man wants to own more than anybody else, everything you can see. The philosophy of late says that he who dies with the most toys wins. This is an example of the influence of these two beasts of Satan.

I heard someone say, "When a man with education meets a man with money, the man with education will walk away with the money and the man with money will walk away with an education." We call that commerce. We call it doing business. When the pride of life and the lust for the things that my eyes can see are combined, a desire to trade and barter and possess occurs. This results in commerce in cities that are filled with desired things and the desire for gain leads people to sell wrong things.

A good example of that today is the internet. I buy and sell a lot on the internet. I can shop on the internet easier than I can go to a store. They always have what I am looking for. I don't have to drive to a major city to find the stores that handle the things that I like. I can sit down at my computer and shop for the best and then order. The internet is a very convenient method of doing commerce. It also soon becomes a mechanism for abusing people and selling evil, solicitous things. The pedophiles are there. The pornographers are there. They are seeking the money that comes from selling things after which people lust. When those two beasts rear their ugly heads, the outcome is commerce. Not that there is anything wrong with commerce in and of itself, but people who are greedy and deceived by the lies that the devil teaches, become the city of Babylon, the mother of harlots and the mother of abominations.

The merchandise is of gold and silver and precious stones, of fine linen and purple and silk and scarlet and all fine wood and all manner of vessels of ivory and all vessels of most precious wood and brass and iron and marble and cinnamon and odors and ointments and frankincense and wine and oil and fine flour and wheat and beef and sheep and horses and chariots and slaves and the souls of men. They bartered and traded. Look at the list. Many of the things on the list are things that we need. Many times our commerce is involved in the trading of things that we really don't need. Finally it trades the souls of men and slaves. This imagery reflects what happens when Satan invades the hearts of men and they begin to follow the teachings of the two beasts. The result is the third beast, which is Babylon, the lust of the flesh, fulfilling the pleasures of the flesh.

The purple that is mentioned was from a dye that was traded during this period of time. Royalty wore purple because they could afford the dye. The dye was imported and was very expensive. The list also speaks of frankincense and ointments and odors. That is the same as the frankincense and myrrh that the wise men brought from the east to give to the baby Jesus. They are very expensive items. We received some frankincense as a gift last Christmas. It came in a little foil pouch and contained two little pieces about the size of the end of my finger. It is supposed to be burnt to make the room smell good. How valuable is that? How essential is that? When my wife thinks the house doesn't smell good she gets a spray bottle and soaks down the house from one end to the other. She paid for an aerosol can to make the place smell like flowers. That is what the commerce is about. It is seeking after those things of this earth which we really don't need, but we want. What am I willing to pay? I am willing to take two jobs. I am willing to work 60 and 70 hours a week. I am willing to save my money so I can have that thing. I am willing to pledge myself with a lot of debt so I can have that thing. I am willing to pay high interest. I am willing to sell myself as a slave. My willingness is based upon my desire for those things I don't really need. That is the beast. That is Babylon. That is the beast of Satan that deceives and enslaves us.

This chapter is not to just describe Babylon, the third beast of Satan. Rather, it is about what happens to Babylon when the judgment comes. The seven bowls which are poured out upon the earth, which are God's wrath and God's judgment, are reflected upon again. The angel asks, if we realize what happened to Babylon. Babylon was overthrown by the Meads and the Persians. What happened to Rome? That great and powerful city of Rome and that great world empire also fell. As they became more and more wicked their military collapsed. They became corrupt and wicked and it destroyed them from within. There is a 12 volume work entitled, "The Rise and Fall of the Roman Empire" that studies the failure of Rome. It is frightening to observe that the things which happened in Rome are happening in America. Rome became cultured and educated. Every man did what was right in his own eyes. The devil seems to repeat this process in every generation. The fall is described as a mighty angel who came down and picked up a huge millstone and threw it into the sea. The resulting tsunami inundated the city of Babylon and the commerce was stopped immediately.

When a nation full of powerful commerce fails, the economy fails soon after. When the Middle East countries went to war and burned their oil refineries, we could not get enough gasoline in the United States. As gasoline become scarce, the price started going up. As the price went up, there comes a price when we will change our habits. We will cease to buy gasoline. It will greatly change our lives because we have become a people dependent on gasoline. My Mom and Dad told me about moving from Hickman County, Tennessee to Gibson County, Tennessee in the early 1900s. They traveled by mules and wagons. They would stop every evening alongside the side of the dirt road and camp. All of their worldly belongings were in the wagons drawn by mules. It took weeks to travel from Hickman County to Gibson County, a trip I now can make in two to three hours. When Babylon falls, commerce will fail. The meat and vegetables won't be able to get to the grocery store. The cantaloupes and tomatoes from Florida will cease. Produce from California will stop. The price and availability of those things will change. It happens quickly. It is not drawn out over many generations. It happens within years. When Rome fell, it was followed by The Dark Ages. When Babylon fell, the Jewish people returned to Israel and tried to rebuild the temple. However, they did not build it with the splendor of the first one. It was not until the time of Herod that the temple received the decoration that it had in Jesus day. When God's judgment comes upon wicked people by the beast, his judgment is swift and real.

When Babylon was destroyed, all of the merchants who did business there and all of the ship masters, who came in and out of the ports, stopped. In verse 17 we read,

> "Every shipmaster, all who travel by ship, sailors, and as many as trade on the sea, stood at a distance."

How many rushed in to rescue? In the Middle East today when Israel entered Lebanon other countries stood off in a distance saying that they ought not to do that. Just like Babylon, they stood afar off and did nothing. They stood afar off, saw the smoke of her burning, threw dust on their head and wept saying,

> "Alas, alas, that great city, in which all who had ships on the sea became rich by her wealth! For in one hour she is made desolate."

God's judgment is swift. God's judgment comes to the wickedness of the earth, as the third beast Babylon, the world of commerce, receives judgment.

The second beast which came from the earth put a mark in our hand so that we could buy and sell. There are efforts in Europe to unify their money system. Several years ago when Carolyn and I traveled in that area we changed our money from the previous country we had visited to the money in the country we were about to visit. In Indonesia, we changed two hundred dollars to rupees and what we received would need a cotton sack to carry it. It was a stack of bills which wouldn't fit in my wallet. It was just two hundred dollars, but it looked like a fortune. When you don't have the mark in your hand, it is hard to do commerce. Recently I bought some bluegrass CD's from Great Britain over the internet. A money service exchanged my dollars for pounds at the current exchange rate and paid for the CD's. We carry the mark in our hand so that we can buy, sell and trade. There is nothing wrong in that except that it leads to buying, selling and trading to the point that our wickedness becomes so full that judgment comes swiftly. When the judgment comes, everybody else stands back and laments.

Recently, I received an email informing me a good friend of mine from work had died that day. I had just talked to the friend last week about helping me with a project. He was 50 years old. When I went to work on Monday I received a notice about his funeral services. However, nothing at work stopped. At the end of the week there were no changes because he was gone. We stand afar off and look at the judgment of God and perhaps even mourn over it, but we soon forget and go on.

The city of Babylon has fallen over and over again in our history; but there will come a time when God will end all commerce. In Verse 22,

> *"The sound of harpists, musicians, flutists, and trumpeters shall not be heard in you anymore. No craftsman of any craft shall be found in you anymore, and the sound of a millstone shall not be heard in you anymore. The light of a lamp shall not shine in you anymore, and the voice of bridegroom and bride shall not be heard in you anymore."*

REVELATION – CHAPTER 19

We have observed several times that this book is not chronological. It is not ordered in time. Jesus gives John a picture of God's planning and providence. We are shown that God will be victorious. The first vision from heaven described Jesus Christ's victory over Satan and the ultimate judgment of the world. Halfway through the book we found the world finished and the story done. In Chapter 12, John sees another sign in heaven and the story begins over again. Why would he start the story over again? It is common in literature and movies to take you back in time. The story line will flash back in time to an appropriate moment to learn what brought you to the present. In Revelation, John is carried back and is shown the same history of the world as viewed through the eyes of men.

To execute the plan of God, Jesus came to the earth to be our perfect advocate. He was tempted in all points as we are. Jesus knows the human perspective of dealing with Satan. Jesus wanted John to understand God's planning from the earthly perspective of the temptations and struggles that would face man during and after the battle with Satan in heaven. In that battle, God cast Satan to the earth. Satan was angry and began to attack the things that were precious to God. He accused the nation of Israel. He accused the Messiah. He thought he was victorious at the crucifixion of Jesus Christ, but Christ was resurrected from the dead. Death had no power over Jesus. As a result, the devil enlists beasts on the earth to deceive and condemn man; a beast that comes out of the sea, a beast that comes out of the earth, and the beast Babylon. These beasts tempt us with the things of this world, the lust of the flesh, the lust of the eyes, and the pride of life.

These beasts are guided by the great dragon, the serpent, Satan. John is shown the judgment that God is going to bring upon those beasts and upon the wicked people who follow after the beasts. God's judgment is pictured in the seven bowls that are poured out upon the earth. John is shown the destruction of the beast from the sea and the beast from the earth and then in reflection the third beast of Babylon.

In chapter 19, the first third of the chapter belongs with chapter 18 and continues with the destruction of Babylon. In chapter 19:1-2 we read,

> *"After these things I heard a loud voice of a great multitude in heaven, saying, 'Alleluia! Salvation and glory and honor and power belong to the Lord our God! For true and righteous are His judgments, because He has judged the great harlot who corrupted the earth with her fornication; and He has avenged on her the blood of His servants shed by her.' Again they said, 'Hallelujah.' Her smoke rises up forever and ever."*

The twenty four-elders and the four living creatures worship God. Then a voice came from the throne saying,

> *"Praise our God, all of you his servants and those who fear Him both small and great."*

The outcome of the destruction of Babylon is rejoicing from the great multitude in heaven. They praise God. Three times in that reading and four times in this chapter the word hallelujah occurs. It occurs in verse 1 verse 3, verse 4 and in verse 6. Remember that we have made the byword of Revelation as "Hallelujah Anyway."

All of the bad things that happen because Satan is making war against God will cease. These multitudes have seen the impact of the war and rejoice in the victory. They say praise the Lord four times. The word hallelujah is an interesting word. In the Old Testament, there is a Hebrew word that means praise the Lord used numerous time. The Book of Psalms is full of the word hallelujah. This word occurs four times in this chapter, but it is the only time this word occurs in the New Testament. This rejoicing is unique in all the New Testament.

In verse 6 it reads,

> *"And I heard, as it were, the voice of a great multitude."*

Here is an interesting observation about interpretation. In verse 1 it reads, "I heard a loud voice of a great multitude." In verse 6, the words "as it were" make a difference in the two readings. The first reading is hearing a multitude; the second is hearing something that sounds like it is coming from a multitude. It is important in the interpretation of prophecy to recognize the things that are figurative as distinct from the things that are literal. Here, there is a distinction made. The best way to understand the difference is to let the Bible instruct you. It is possible to make figurative images of all kinds of things. As a preacher, I have to be very careful even when studying a parable to not take the parallels too far. The purpose of the parable has to be kept paramount. If not, it is possible to take the parable and make applications that may or may not be correct. However, the application that Jesus makes of the parable is the reason He told the story. It is the same way with these prophecies. In this instance, it does not really matter a lot, but we should understand that in one case John heard a multitude and in the other case, he heard something that *sounded* like a multitude.

He continues in verse 6 with,

> *"... as the sound of many waters and as the sound of mighty thundering."*

John heard something and attempted to describe it. Have you ever been in a thunderstorm and heard a great peal of thunder that goes rampant across the sky. Somebody said, "God is bowling." You can hear that huge bowling ball rolling across the sky. It sounds like somebody bowling, but it isn't. This sounded like a great multitude or mighty thunder or the surf at the ocean.

When I lived in Florida we would often surf fish on the beach. We stood in the waves as they were breaking so we could cast the bait past the breakers and catch fish. One of the memories of that was how loud the ocean sounded. As the waters rolled in and beat the sandy beach and the wind whistled and blew; it was noisy. You could not hear somebody a few feet down the beach talking. The sound

John heard was like mighty waters and like thunder. The loud noise was the sound of saying, "Hallelujah." Not only are these multitudes of people saying it, but John is hearing the heavenly hosts. The mountains shout and the trees cry out the praise of God. John is hearing it everywhere around him. He is inundated with the sound. While in Florida, I had the opportunity to see the launch of Apollo 13 when the astronauts were going to the moon. My older brother was the deputy director of the Apollo launch vehicle program at NASA in Huntsville. He got my wife and I VIP (very important persons) seats. The VIP seats were at the vertical assembly building right in front of the launch pad. We were three miles from the pad and could see the Apollo rocket on the pad. We were sitting on bleachers with senators and famous people. We were rubbing shoulders with the VIP's and watching the launch. Apollo 13 was the one moon mission that never made it to the moon. It was the one they made the movie about. I was so disappointed when they did not make it to the moon, but this mission became the most famous. The thing that I remember most about that rocket launch was the sound. The sound was so loud and so deep that it was as though something was beating against my chest in a slow rhythm. Just as that set of explosions rocketed the astronauts into the sky, I imagined John surrounded by the heavenly hosts and those who have been resurrected as they praise God. This is victory. This is victory over sins. This is victory over evil and wickedness. They say hallelujah; for the Lord God omnipotent reigns. Let us be glad and rejoice and give him glory. *4 Times*

The remainder of the chapter's content speaks of the marriage of the Lamb. His wife has made herself ready and to her it was granted to be arrayed in fine linen. The linen is clean and bright for it is the righteous acts of the saints. We are introduced to the bride and groom. A Jewish marriage is not like an American marriage. The marriage in a Jewish community was arranged. It was not a matter of you deciding who you wanted to marry. It was your parents who decided who you were to marry. You would be betrothed and the groom would have to pay a dowry to the father of the girl. In the Jewish community the groom gave a dowry at the time of betrothal and the bride was espoused to the groom until marriage. Recall that Mary was espoused to Joseph when she became pregnant with Jesus. During the espousal, they were considered marriage partners, but they did not live together. It was a time when they were allowed to get to know each other since the marriage was arranged. During this engagement period, it was considered the same as marriage except for the conjugal relationship. Finally, the marriage would be consummated at a feast. Everybody who came to the marriage feast would stay for several days.

Notice how this marriage of the Lamb is so similar. There was a betrothal in the marriage of the Lamb and there was a dowry that Jesus paid. He paid the dowry with his own blood. We are not bought with the blood of bulls and goats, but with the precious blood of the Lamb; a Lamb without spots or blemish. The price of the bride of Christ is the ultimate price. It is the death of the Lamb of God, a Lamb who was spotless, innocent and perfect. Obviously Jesus is the groom in this marriage, but who is the bride? The bride is the church. The church in the Bible is referred to as the Bride of Christ. We call ourselves the Church of Christ on the sign outside the building but we could just as easily put the Bride of Christ on the sign. It is a Bible name for the church. The Bride of Christ, the church of Christ is a reasonable way to shows that we belong to Christ. We have been betrothed and we are in that period when we are getting to know each other. We are espoused. The marriage relationship will be consummated at the marriage supper that Revelation chapter 19 describes. In 2 Corinthians 11:2 we read,

> *"For I am jealous for you with godly jealousy. For I have betrothed you to one husband, that I may present you as a chaste virgin to Christ."*

Those words are marriage words that relate how the Jews would see the relationship between God and his church as a relationship between a man and his wife. In Ephesians chapter 5, we read that women are to submit themselves to their husband as unto the Lord and that the husband is to love his wife like Christ loved the church and gave himself for it. Paul ends that discourse by saying that he speaks in a mystery for he speaks of Christ and His church. In Hosea 2:19 the same idea is spoken of as God being betrothed to His people

John is told to write,

> *"Blessed are those who are called to the marriage supper of the Lamb!"*

When we began the Book of Revelation we saw that there were seven blesseds, seven beatitudes in the Book of Revelation. This is number four. Four hallelujah's and four beatitudes ought to be easy to remember. Blessed are those who are called to the marriage supper of the Lamb. Jesus gave a parable about a wedding feast where the man who was giving the feast sent out invitations and people began to make excuses. Well, blessed are those who are called to the marriage feast of the Lamb and don't make excuses.

The angel said to John,

> *"These are the true sayings of God,"*

And John fell at the angel's feet to worship him. The angel said,

> *"See that you do not do that! I am your fellow servant, and of your brethren who have the testimony of Jesus. Worship God! For the testimony of Jesus is the spirit of prophecy."*

Imagine the thundering noise and the imposing angel. It is an emotional time and John is overwhelmed. He falls to his knees. He bows down before this angel. The angel replies,

> *"I am your fellow servant, and of your brethren."*

Are the angels our brothers? Sometimes children ask, "When you die and go to heaven will you be an angel?" I believe the answer is yes. God's spiritual creation was created by God and filled with

His spirit. When God formed us from the dust of the earth, He breathed into our nostrils the breath, the spirit of life, and we became a living creature. We possess a part of God, a part that returns to God who gave it (Ecclesiastics 9). Our spirit has the abilities and powers of a spirit; of an angel. The angel refuses John's worship because he is his brother. He is one of the multitudes that are praising God. He says I am your fellow servant, your brother, who hath the testimony of Jesus. He says to worship God, for the testimony of Jesus is the spirit of prophecy. In the beginning of this study, we noted that to understand we need to put Jesus in it. Jesus, when on this earth encouraged the people to search the scriptures because the scriptures are where you learn about Jesus, they testify of Him. The angel said the testimony of Jesus is the spirit of prophecy. When modern day prophets talk about Israel and the temple and an earthly kingdom and earthly things, just remember that if it is not about Jesus, it isn't out of God's word. If it is not about Jesus, it is the figment of someone's imagination. For Jesus is King of Kings and Lord of Lords.

In chapter 19 we see Jesus pictured again. There are several portraits of Jesus in the Book of Revelation. We do not have any physical pictures of Jesus as he lived on this earth. Artists have rendered their pictures of Jesus, but the ones I have seen look like an Anglo Saxon and not like someone who was Jewish during the first century. We do not know what Jesus looked like. In that time the Jews considered it idolatry to make any kind of an image of a human. The Jews despised the busts and statues that the Romans made. So we have no pictures of what Jesus looked like as a man. However, we have many pictures of what Jesus looks like as the Son of God. In Chapter 1 we saw a heavenly image of Jesus and in Revelation Chapter 19 is another.

In verse 11-16 John describes,

"Now I saw heaven opened, and behold a white horse. And He who sat on him was called Faithful and True, and in righteousness He judges and makes war. His eyes were like a flame of fire, and on His head were many crowns. He had a name written that no one knew except Himself. He was clothed with a robe dipped in blood, and His name is called The Word of God. And the armies in heaven, clothed in fine linen, white and clean, followed Him on white horses. Now out of His mouth goes a sharp sword, that with it He should strike the nations. And He Himself will rule them with a rod of iron. He Himself treads the winepress of the fierceness and wrath of Almighty God. And He has on His robe and on His thigh a name written: KING OF KINGS AND LORD OF LORDS."

The picture never reveals that it is Jesus, but the angel has already said in the verse just before that the testimony of Jesus is the spirit of prophecy. The angel says it is about Jesus and the word picture of Jesus is then portrayed. He is on a white horse. O you remember the four horsemen in Revelation chapter 5. I suggested that the rider on the white horse was Jesus. Here is the reason for believing it was Jesus. We see Him appearing again on a white horse and this time we have no doubt that it is Jesus for He is King of Kings and Lord of Lords. He rules with a rod of iron. We see the sword coming out of his mouth. We have already seen that once before. We saw the sword coming out of His mouth in Revelation 1. The Hebrew writer says the word of God is like a sharp two-edged sword cutting going and coming. It pierces even to separate the bones and the marrow and the soul and the spirit. It is also this great sword that is the only offensive weapon in the arsenal of the Christian recorded in Ephesians 6. Ephesians 6 describes the armor of the Christian soldier. Paul said to put on a helmet of salvation, have your loins girded with truth, our feet shod with the preparation of the gospel of peace, the breastplate of righteousness. These are all defensive. Then, he adds the sword of the spirit, which is the word of God. It is God's word that does battle. It is God's word that slays the enemy. It is God's word that is the power to overcome Satan.

His eyes were like a flame of fire; on His head were many crowns. He had a name written that no one knew except Himself. A little later, His name is called the Word of God, and on His robe and on His thigh a name written King of Kings and Lord of Lords. There are three references to a name here in this set of verses. The first is a name written that no one knows. The second one is the Word of God, and the third one is King of Kings and Lord of Lords. Someone might ask what the right name for the church is. We have a sign that reads church of Christ. That is a scriptural name. The Bible uses that name for the church in Romans 16:16. But the church could also be called the bride of Christ as we have discussed. We could also refer to it as Christ's church because it belongs to Him. It is the one He built. The church of Christ can go by different names, but those names should have meaning. When Abram received the promise of God, God changed his name to Abraham. When Sarai became the mother of all living, her name was changed to Sarah. When Jacob was no longer a supplanter and recognized his need for God, he became the prince of all nations and God named him Israel. Throughout the Bible, God places importance on names. In the Jewish mind, names convey heritage. Today we place great importance in the names of our children. In marriage, the bride takes the name of her husband. This vision reinforces that God is serious about names.

Jesus had a name written which no one knew. It is not referring to the Word of God or King of Kings and Lord of Lords because we know those. It is another name that has not been revealed. It is something about Jesus that has not been revealed to us. It is like the new song we are going to sing. We don't know what it is. God still has things in store for us. Do you wonder what we'll do in heaven? I know we are going to be praising God, but what else? Would you believe that we are going to fight in heaven? Isn't it a place of peace? Revelation 19 speaks about being at war. In the end time Jesus is looking like a commander, and the armies of heaven are clothed in fine linen and white and clean. What was this army doing? They were going to battle with Jesus. The faithful are going to be a part of the victory. We are going to be victorious over Satan.

Jesus riding on His white horse has His army behind Him. His army is they who are clothed in white linen. In the first vision those in white linen referred to those who were chosen out of the world to have their garments washed in the blood of the Lamb. Jesus' garment is dipped in blood. We have read about the fierceness of God's wrath against those who are wicked. How those who are evil are put in the winepress and beat out until the blood flows high and far. Jesus is reaping victory. He is the one who is the judge. We see His blood cleansing His army and the blood of the wicked slain on His garment.

In verse 17 we learn more about the marriage feast.

"Then I saw an angel standing in the sun; and he cried with a loud voice, saying to all the birds that fly in the midst of heaven, 'Come and gather together for the supper of the great God,'"

The angel invites all to gather for the supper of the great God that you may eat the flesh of kings, the flesh of captains, the flesh of mighty men, the flesh of horses and those who sit on them and the flesh of all people free and slave, both small and great. Jesus said in Matthew 24 concerning the destruction of Jerusalem in that judgment against the Jews who rejected Him, that when you see the birds you will know. These birds likewise mark another day of the Lord as Jesus brings judgment to the wicked of this world. These birds are being called to the supper of the flesh of those who have been wicked and have been judged unrighteous by God.

"And I saw the beast, the kings of the earth, and their armies, gathered together to make war against Him who sat on the horse and against His army." There is going to be a battle. A great battle is going to occur between those who are righteous, those who are following the white horse of the Lamb of God and those who are of the beast and those who are of the earth. Then the beast was captured and with him the false prophet, whose miracles deceived those who received the mark of the beast and those who worshiped his image. These two were cast alive into the lake of fire burning with brimstone. The rest were killed with the sword which proceeded from the mouth of Him who sat on the horse, and all of the birds were filled with their flesh. The marriage supper of the Lamb is a battle, the Battle of Armageddon.

Why are the beasts left alive when they are cast into the bottomless pit and all of their followers are killed? I don't know, but I have a guess. The beasts were spiritual beings while those who followed them are physical beings. For the physical, it is appointed unto man once to die and after that, the judgment. The wages of sin is death. There is no doubt that those who sin will suffer death and pass to the Hadean realm of Luke 16. Then in chapter 20 Christ will call the spirits out of Hades for judgment. Ultimately, they will be judged, but they must first die. When they are cast into the lake of fire it is referred to as the second death. The beast is cast in alive because he is a spiritual being already. However, those who are physical must die in order to become, spiritual immortal beings able to face the judgment.

In Revelation 17:14, it says that the beast will make war with the Lamb. The Lamb will overcome them for he is the Lord of Lords and King of Kings. Those who are with him are called chosen and faithful. Who was it that was with him? It was the chosen and the faithful. Those that were with him and the Lamb Jesus were going to battle. In Revelation 16:14 it says,

111

"For they are spirits of demons, performing signs, which go out to the kings of the earth and of the whole world, to gather them to the battle of that great day of God Almighty."

It again refers to the battle of God Almighty.

"Behold, I am coming as a thief. Blessed is he who watches, and keeps his garments, lest he walk naked and they see his shame. And they gathered them together to the place called in Hebrew, Armageddon."

Armageddon is that last great battle, the one portrayed in Revelation Chapter 19. When you read Chapter 16, you see there is a battle. In Chapter 17 you see there is a battle. In Chapter 19 you see there is a battle. You would think there are a lot of battles, but they all refer to the same battle. John is dealing with how God's judgment is to progress in relation to all the enemies. When the beasts are being discussed John tells of the battle he will fight. When Babylon is being described John says she is going to lose her fight. There is going to be a battle with Babylon. In Chapter 19 as Jesus who wages the war against Satan, it is apparent that these are all the same battle.

When we were reading about Christ on the white horse in verse 11 the word "was" is in italics. In verse 12, His eyes were and the word "were" is also in italics. The italics mean these words were not in the original text but were added by the translators. All of the words are past tense. It could just as easily be present or future. The idea being conveyed is that the King of Kings and Lord of Lords and His eternal nature is and will always be victorious over Satan.

Hallelujah, hallelujah, hallelujah and hallelujah because the beast from the sea, the beast from the earth and that great dragon and the terrible city Babylon are all going to come under the judgment of the Lamb. Those who are righteous and chosen will be rejoicing at the marriage supper of the Lamb. Birds will gather to feast upon the flesh of all of those physical who have turned their backs on God. This is neither a pretty picture nor a very popular idea, but it is the truth that God will judge the wicked. There will come a time when people will reap the consequences of their behavior. We want to be in the army that is chosen and faithful, following Him riding a white horse and wearing linen clothing that has been washed in the blood of the Lamb. It is most important. It is eternal. It represents God's opportunity that we have to be saved from the destruction that is brought about by the wickedness of Satan upon the earth.

REVELATION - CHAPTER 20

"Then I saw an angel coming down from heaven, having the key to the bottomless pit and a great chain in his hand."

This chapter has only 15 verses, but they are the source of great discussion, dispute, and controversy among Bible scholars. These verses have produced very differing thoughts. We will attempt to present some of these approaches as a springboard for further study. After being made aware of the multitude of interpretations we will be better prepared to study for ourselves and reach our own conclusions.

These verses are one of the major sources of an area of study called eschatology. This big word is a combination of two Greek words that mean study and last together becoming a study of the end time. Some things in these verses are not mentioned anywhere else in the scriptures. For instance, the thousand years is only mentioned here. The terms first resurrection and second death also catch our imagination. Below is a table of some relevant eschatology scriptures.

Matthew 25:31-46	Sheep and Goat Judgment
I Thessalonians 4:13-18	"Rapture" (actually from Latin translation for "caught up")
II Thessalonians 2:1-12	Man of sin (Antichrist?)
I John 2:18	Antichrist
Revelation 16:16	Battle of Armageddon
Revelation 20:1-10	Binding of Satan Thousand years (Millennium) Satan Loosed First resurrection Gog and Magog
Revelation 20:11-15	Great White Throne Judgment
Revelation 7:14	Great Tribulation
Matthew 24:21	Erroneously used also to speak of the alleged "Great Tribulation" at the end of the world. These verses are still in answer to Jesus question about the destruction of the temple at the destruction of Jerusalem in 70 AD. See verse 34 as the transition from the first question to the second.

The thousand years in chapter 20 is often called the millennium. The debates about the millennium can be divided into four major camps. Each millennial theory has to do with how the 1,000 years (millennium) relates to the other end time events that are recorded in the scriptures. The four approaches are named historical premillennialism, dispensational premillennialism, postmillennialism, and amillinnialism. All but the last one of these approaches picture a utopian literal 1,000 year reign of Christ on this earth.

The most popular approach today is dispensational premillennialism. Dispensational premillennialism had its origin among the Plymouth Brethren in Ireland and England in the early 19th century. It was conceived and expounded by John Nelson Darby (1800-1882) who was one of the chief founders of the Plymouth Brethren and was a reaction against the Church of England's view of postmillennialism. These teachings spread widely in Canada and the United States due to the printing of the 1909 Scofield Reference Bible. This approach is held by several popular television evangelists and has been the basis for several books of fiction and movies depicting the end time.

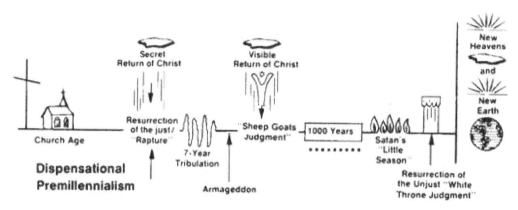

Dispensational premillennialists view God's dealings with humanity in dispensations or period of time when man is tested in some particular aspect of God's will. They believe the Jewish dispensation of the Old Testament to promise the Jews an earthly kingdom ruled by the Messiah. Christ came and offered this kingdom to the Jews but they rejected it. This kingdom was then postponed until some point in the future and Christ established the church in its stead. At the end of this church age God will rapture all believers, exclusive of Old Testament saints, and they will go to heaven to celebrate with Christ, "the marriage feast of the Lamb," for seven years. During this seven year period (Revelation 6-19), there will be a tribulation, the Antichrist will reign, and terrible judgments will fall on the earth. A remnant of Israel (the 144,000 of Revelation 7) will believe in Jesus as the Messiah and preach the gospel and a multitude of Gentiles will be saved. Near the end of the seven years, a number of military battles will take place leading up to the Battle of Armageddon. At this time, Christ (together with the church) returns and destroys His enemies. The majority of the Israelites will be saved, and Satan will be bound for 1,000 years. Believers who have died during the tribulation and the Old Testament saints will be raised and join the earthly kingdom. Christ will judge the living Gentiles (Matt. 25:31-46); the "goats" will be cast into hell. The "sheep" and the believing Jews still living will enter the millennium in their natural bodies and marry, reproduce, and die. The millennium will be a golden age of prosperity and peace. Worship will center around the rebuilt temple. At the beginning of the millennium only believers will be left on earth but some of their offspring will not believe. Satan will gather these unbelievers in one last revolt (Rev. 20:7-9). Toward the end, all believers who die during the millennium will be raised. After Satan's "little season," all the unbelieving dead will then be raised and judged. (Rev. 20:11-15) The new heaven and earth will then begin.

In contrast, the historic premillennialists believe that Christ's second coming will be all at once after the tribulation. They believe that the vast majority of Jews will have been converted. Believers who have died will be raised, those alive will be transformed, and all believers will meet Christ in the air and then descend with Him to earth. Christ will kill the Antichrist, bind Satan, and set up His 1,000 year reign on earth. Christ and His redeemed, both Jews and Gentiles, will reign over the unbelieving nations still on earth. People in resurrected bodies and natural bodies will live together on the earth. Sin and death will still exist, but external evil will be restrained. The 1,000 years of Christ's earthly kingdom will be a time of social, political, and economic justice and great prosperity. After these 1,000 years, Satan will be loosed in order to deceive the unbelieving nations into making a final assault against the redeemed. Satan will be destroyed and cast into the lake of fire. The dead unbelievers will be resurrected and all will be judged. This is followed by the new heaven and earth. Historical Premillennialists trace the history of this view back to writings of early church fathers such as Polycarp and Ignatius.

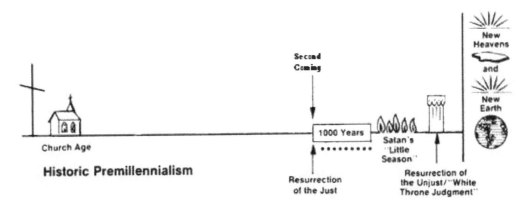

The less common postmillennial view expects Christ's second coming after (post) the millennium. After Christ's coming, the rapture, the general resurrection, the general judgment, and the new heaven and earth occur. This view does not involve a visible reign of Christ in an earthly form, nor is the millennial period literally a 1,000 years. However, the postmillennial view does expect a recognizable millennial period which is a golden age of prosperity and peace among all. They believe this period will occur gradually under the increasing influence of Christianity, leading to the reduction of evil and to greatly improved conditions in the social, economic, political and cultural spheres. They believe that the entire world will eventually be Christianized to the point that the Christian belief and value system will become standard for all nations.

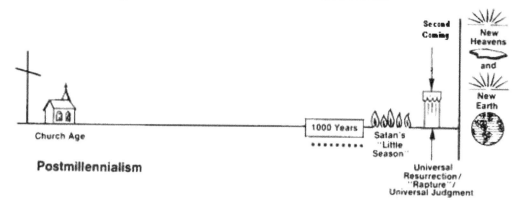

The fourth of these approaches does not teach a literal thousand-year earthly reign of Christ is called amillinnialism. Those who adhere to this approach believe that the thousand-year reference is a figurative expression for the present reign of Christ which began upon His ascension into heaven and will be fully manifested at His second coming. Christ's second coming will be one event at which time He will raise up the dead and living and give unto all believer's eternal life.

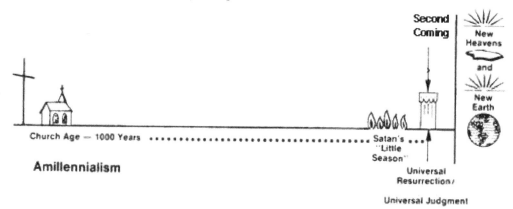

How do these views align with careful analysis of all the revealed features of the end time and knowledge of the nature of God and His promises? As far as a millennium is concerned we have direct scriptural reference to the thousand year reign of Christ in this chapter. There can be no disagreement about that. The differences arise in how these and the aforementioned end time verses are interpreted. While the approaches differ about how and when the return of Christ will be, they all agree that he will return visibly in person and they all hope for the glorious appearing of the great God and our Savior Jesus Christ. They all believe that the Lord himself shall descend from heaven with a shout, with the voice of an archangel, and with the trump of God. They all agree that when He comes he will raise the dead, execute judgment and begin eternity.

However, the millennium anticipated by each of these views is quite different not only in how and when it will be set up, but also in the nature of the kingdom and how Christ will exercise his control. Premillennialists envision an earthy reign of Jesus even though nowhere in the scriptures is it taught. To be one you must believe that the kingdom of God has nothing to do with eternity; that the church was established as an afterthought because the Jews rejected Jesus; and that the temple will be rebuilt; that the temple priesthood will be restarted; and that the failed mission of Christ must be redone. To fit their chronological interpretation of Revelation, they require belief in multiple resurrections and multiple judgments.

To be a dispensationalist you must additionally believe that there is a different way for Jews to be saved than Gentiles. They use a literal interpretation of the Old Testament promises and fit the New Testament into it. They anticipate the rapture of the saved dead before the millennium and the resurrection of the unsaved dead after the millennium. They invent the word rapture from the Latin which does not occur in our English Bible to justify multiple resurrections making a distinction between rising and being caught up. They require three judgments; one of the believer's works at the rapture, one at the second coming for physical Israel, and one after the millennium for the unsaved dead.

The postmillennialist don't teach the earthy reign of Jesus, but do believe that the church age will grow into a world of peace ruled by Christians. If you look at the history of the world, it is difficult to imagine it getting better and better and better, but this theory requires it for their thousand year reign.

All three of these theories accept the millennium as a literal 1,000 years in spite of the fact that most of the numbers in Revelation are not literal. From our numerology review we remember the number 10 representing completeness. After all, the number 10 would count all the fingers and thumbs and is used as the base of their and our number system. Adding the Hebrew superlative idea already discussed, the most complete time would be imagined as 10x10x10=1,000. So, when I view this number 1,000, I don't see it as a literal number. It is rather a most complete period of time and is used to describe the church age. It is the age we live in now. Jesus said "and lo, I am with you always, even to the end of the age." This is the age in which He reigns. He is reigning in heaven until He puts all things under His feet. He has no reason to come back to the earth.

The scriptures teach one second coming, one resurrection from the dead and one judgment. The millennium is figurative language representing the church age. Satan is bound because his powers are limited (see Jude 6). The reign of Christ is spiritual and is going on right now. When He comes again He will not set a foot on earth for we will meet Him in the air. There will be no earthly kingdom, but Jesus will turn the spiritual kingdom, which already exists over to God (1 Corinthians 15:20-28).

This scripture speaks of a first resurrection which implies more than one resurrection and hence the numerous theories of the premillennialists and the doctrine of the rapture. However, to those of us who believe that the millennium is the church age the first resurrection simply occurs as the Bible describes in Romans 6 when the old man of sin dies, we bury him in baptism and as Jesus rose from the dead, we too rise from that watery grave of baptism to walk in newness of life. We become a new spiritual creature. We experience the first resurrection in our spiritual life and experience a second resurrection from the grave (Hades) when Christ comes again. Those who are saved by baptism will still die a physical death, but because they are saved, but they will never have to experience the second death of eternal separation from God in outer darkness in the lake of fire. Those saved by this baptism (first resurrection) are added by God to the church (kingdom) and become rulers with Christ.

During the church age (figurative 1,000 years) Satan is bound in a bottomless pit for the whole age. There are references throughout Revelation that describe Satan as the deceiver of nations. However, he can no longer deceive those who resist in the church age because he has been bound. The blood of Jesus and the testimony of His word bind Satan. We have the revealed will of God to turn away his temptations. Jesus set the example for us when Satan tempted Him. Jesus responded to each temptation with the words "It is written." Christ used this same approach even when Satan attempted to misinterpret the scriptures. At the end of the church age Satan is released for a little season and deceives the lost world to participate in the battle of Armageddon. We have looked at this battle in chapters 16, 17, and 19. They are all parallels of what is described in chapter 20.

This following picture illustrates the history of Satan recorded in the Bible and helps to understand what is recorded in chapter 20. We read about Satan the very first time in the Garden of Eden, tempting Eve. Satan was in heaven during that time. We read in the Book of Job, which is probably the oldest book in the Old Testament, about Satan in heaven meeting with the sons of God who are those spiritual beings created by God. Satan was described as walking to and fro upon the earth. Satan had the ability to be in heaven and to be on earth. Throughout the history of the Old Testament, Satan was involved in things on the earth, but at the cross Satan was cast out of heaven. With Jesus victory over death, the power of sin (death) was removed and the devil was bound. The devil was overcome and he was cast into the bottomless pit. The millennium began and Satan has been bound since. All he now has to deceive the world are his beasts and death which remain.

Satan in Revelation

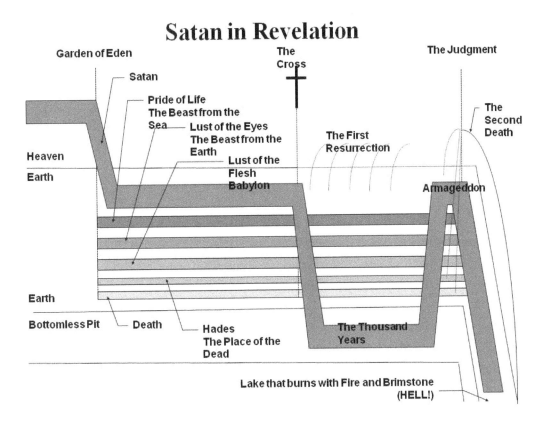

He will be released at the time of the end and Armageddon will occur. In this great battle, Satan, Gog and Magog will fight against the armies of God and be ultimately defeated. Satan and all his followers will suffer a second death (separation from God). Satan and his followers will be thrown in a lake that burns with fire and brimstone, which in other places is referred to as Hell. There are also three beasts in the picture. The beast from the sea, the beast from the earth and Babylon are shown on the earth. Also pictured is the place of the dead and death itself. They are going to be delivered up in the judgment described in this chapter. Death and Hades were created after the sin in the Garden of Eden.

During the time of Jesus miracles were performed on people who were afflicted by Satan when he took over their bodies. There are certainly people today who have the influence of Satan in their lives, but it is a matter of choice. We choose to allow Satan to have an influence in our lives. Prior to the death of Jesus there was a time when that was not true. Recall in the story of Job, how Satan was granted the power to take those things from Job that were his, even to the slaying of his children. Satan had that power because God granted it to him. Satan was later granted the power to even touch Job's health. God controls the limitations that are placed upon Satan. What are the limitations on Satan today? This scripture says he can deceive the nations no more. Nations are deceived when they choose to follow the beasts of Satan. If we resist him, he will flee from us. He has no power except what we allow.

The parallel accounts of the battle of Armageddon in Chapters 16, 17 and 19 are all provided to show God's judgment on every aspect of evil. Evil is completely defeated and none of it will enter heaven. As John writes, He is using flashback like an author writing a novel. All the characters and all the subplots are being dealt with so we get the complete picture. These flashbacks reset the timeline to allow revelation of how God is victorious over all that is evil.

Near the end of chapter 19, John wrote of the marriage supper of the Lamb. However, this marriage supper was not what you might imagine. It was not a feast. It was rather a victorious battle over Christ's enemies. He succeeds in the final victory over Satan and the beasts that Satan has brought to influence our lives today. The tools of Satan on the earth, the lust of the flesh, the lust of the eyes, the pride of life portrayed as the beast of the sea, the beast from the earth and Babylon are defeated.

Beginning in verse 11, after the victory over evil, there is a judgment that we refer to as the great white throne judgment. It is also described in Mathew chapter 25 where Jesus separates the sheep and the goats. This illustrates that unlike some of the theories which teach numerous resurrections there will be only one with both the righteous and the wicked present. There are lost, sinful people and there are people who have been washed in the blood of the Lamb at the judgment. We also see both the righteous and wicked present at the second coming as Paul wrote to the brethren at Thessalonica. He encouraged them to comfort one another with the fact that those who die are still going to be called into the judgment and will not be delayed by the living. The dead will rise first and then the living will follow. Note that both the living and the dead will meet Him in the air. There is never a reference to Jesus setting foot on this earth again.

Because this is referred to as a judgment may well up a mistaken idea in our modern minds. Our lives are judged minute by minute as God writes in His book of memory and as the blood of Jesus writes our names in the book of life. This judgment is the reading of these entries in the book, checking the book of life, and passing the sentence of both the good and evil to their eternal destiny. We are assured that we are saved by the blood of Jesus each day that we live in Him. At the judgment there are pleas and explanations but this event is about the formal sentencing. In Luke 16, in the story of the rich man and Lazarus, after they died they immediately knew their destiny. As soon as they died they were either in paradise or torment. Likewise the thief on the cross was told by Jesus that He would be with him in paradise that day. Thus judgment is known at death. Hebrews 9:27 teaches,

"And as it is appointed for men to die once, but after this the judgment."

Judgment occurs after death. This Great White Throne Judgment as it is known is for the sentencing after judgment has already been made. All there will be allowed final words and there will be explanations and excuses, but no appeals. Jesus said in Mathew 25, that when those are separated as goats He explained to them,

"For I was hungry and you gave Me no food; I was thirsty and you gave Me no drink; I was a stranger and you did not take Me in, naked and you did not clothe Me, sick and in prison and you did not visit Me."

The condemned responded,

"Lord, when did we see You?"

Jesus answers them,

"Inasmuch as you did not do it to one of the least of these, you did not do it to Me."

In Matthew 7, Jesus teaches,

"Many will say to Me in that day, 'Lord, Lord, have we not prophesied in Your name, cast out demons in Your name, and done many wonders in Your name?' And then I will declare to them, 'I never knew you; depart from Me, you who practice lawlessness!"

The judged can plead, but sentence will be passed.

"Then I saw a great white throne and Him who sat on it, from whose face the earth and the heaven fled away. And there was found no place for them."

Why was there no place for the heavens and the earth? Because Peter tells us that they are going to be burned up in a fervent heat. Everything on this earth is going to be destroyed when Jesus comes again.

"And I saw the dead, small and great, standing before God."

It was only the dead because all the living at this point have died. The earth has burned up and all those who were living have been changed (1 Corinthians 15), and the mortal have put on immortality. It is appointed unto all men to die so all will be dead to this physical world at the judgment.

"And books were opened. And another book was opened, which is the Book of Life. And the dead were judged according to their works, by the things which were written in the books."

The dead are judged out of the books. God keeps books. He has records in heaven of our lives, the things we do and the things we are involved with. Those books are opened and they provide the testimony that blesses or condemns. We will know as we are known. We will remember and give account of the things recorded in the books. I sometimes forget things. Sometimes, I don't remember; but at the judgment, I will remember and will be judged according to the works which are written in the books.

In verse 13, the sea gave up their dead which were in it and death and Hades delivered up the dead who were in them. We have noted before that the sea represents the multitudes of people. We have also noted in the story of the rich man and Lazarus that those who die go to Hades, the place of the dead. So the sea (living people) die and the dead in Hades and death itself are delivered to the throne. Note that the King James Bible sometimes translates the word Hades as Hell so we confuse it with that place where the wicked reside for eternity. Hades is the word which means grave or place of the dead. It is the same as the Old Testament Hebrew word "sheol" which translates into the word grave or pit. Therefore, when we read that the dead come forth from their grave, it is describing the dead coming forth from Hades and not out of the grave yard. The body in the grave yard returns to the earth which gave it. When we think about the dead rising from their graves, it is the grave where the spirit goes called Hades.

> *"The sea gave up the dead which were in it. Death and Hades delivered up the dead who were in them and they were judged each one according to his works."*

> *"For by grace you have been saved through faith, and that not of yourselves; it is the gift of God, not of works, lest anyone should boast."*

When the judgment occurs, the Judge opens the books and reviews our works written in the books. However, our salvation is dependent on the Book of Life, not the works written in the books. Whether we are saved or are lost, whether we are a sheep or a goat depends on whether we are in Christ or not. Whether we are in Jesus and whether we are walking in the light.

> *There is no condemnation to those who are in Christ and walking in the light (Romans 8:1; 1 John 1:7).*

Those in Christ have their names written in the Book of Life and their works are written in books. Then, what is the judgment by works? Works are certainly important since faith without works is dead. Faith is measured by its works. We are God's workmanship, created unto good works.

As Jesus talks about the judgment in Matthew 25, He tells a parable about a man who was given five talents. He worked and earned five talents more. The Lord said "Well done, good and faithful servant." Another man had two talents. He worked and gained two talents more. The Lord said, "Well done, good and faithful servant." A third man had one talent and he buried it. The Lord said, "You wicked and slothful servant." This story teaches that how much you are given determines how much is expected. God has expectations of us and He will measure us to those expectations.

In 1 Corinthians 3:9-15:

> *"For we are God's fellow workers; you are God's field, you are God's building. According to the grace of God which was given to me, as a wise master builder I have laid the foundation, and another builds on it. But let each one take heed how he*

builds on it. For no other foundation can anyone lay than that which is laid, which is Jesus Christ. Now if anyone builds on this foundation with gold, silver, precious stones, wood, hay, straw, each one's work will become clear; for the Day will declare it, because it will be revealed by fire; and the fire will test each one's work, of what sort it is. If anyone's work which he has built on it endures, he will receive a reward. If anyone's work is burned, he will suffer loss; but he himself will be saved, yet so as through fire."

Paul begins by observing that we are God's fellow laborers. Paul is writing about our labor, our works. We are God's field, we are God's building. By the grace of God, Paul became a wise master builder who has built on the foundation of Jesus. Paul laid the foundation when he preached Jesus and we believed, but we build our building on the foundation. Paul warns we should take heed how we build to be sure we are on the right foundation, for no other foundation can anyone lay than Jesus Christ. In other words, there is no way to be saved except by building on the foundation of Jesus Christ. Building on the foundation keeps our names in the Book of Life. However, we build on the foundation with gold, silver, precious stone, wood, hay and straw. Each one's work will be tested. The day will declare it. There will come a day when God will judge how I built my house on the foundation of Jesus. The fire will test each man's work what sort it is. If any man's work, which he has built on, endures, he will receive a reward. The judgment of works is about how I have done in this life building my temple on the foundation of Jesus Christ. My building will be judged by the works. I will lose all of the things that are ungodly in my building. I am not going to take the bad things into heaven, but the good things I will. If any man's work is burned, he will suffer loss, but, he himself will be saved. I am saved because I am on the foundation and my building is to be judged as through fire.

In the white throne judgment God will measure our works out of the books and provide rewards based on our works. Does that mean some people get more rewards than others? I believe so. Why? Because to whom much is given, much is expected. Will that make the people who get less sad? No, because I will have all that I have the capacity to appreciate. In high school, I was in the band and learned to play classical music by composers like Wagner and Shostakovich, and many names that I could not pronounce. It was not rock and roll. However, I learned to appreciate the beauty of that music. Today when somebody plays rock and roll it rattles my nerves so badly I cannot stay. I don't like it. There are people who really like Rock and Roll. When they like it, it doesn't take anything away from me. That is the way it is going to be in heaven. The works I have done, the things I have learned are going to help me enjoy the spiritual blessings of heaven. God will fill me with those things I appreciate from my spiritual training. That is my reward. You might not get what I get. You don't like what I like. I won't be playing baseball. Some of you may have baseball all day. The things that I have done that are evil are going to be burned up. The good things that I have done are going to be preserved and I will be rewarded according to my works.

Death and Hades were cast into the lake of fire. This is the second death. Having died once physically, the wicked die a second time when their spirit is removed from the presence of God for eternity. There will be no more death. Those who have experienced the first resurrection will not face the second death. Anyone not found written in the Book of Life was cast into the lake of fire. It is eternally important to have your name written in the Book of Life. Make sure you are building your spiritual house on the only foundation, the foundation of the Lamb, the King, the Savior, and the Lord Jesus Christ.

REVELATION – CHAPTER 21

The Book of Revelation is a complex book. It is a book filled with imagery. In the study of the last chapter we saw how much confusion a literal translation of these symbols and images has produced. The one verse I would pick that really brings to light how we ought to look at the Book of Revelation says that the spirit of prophecy is Jesus Christ. We must look for Jesus in Revelation. We have seen Jesus already on a white horse at the beginning. We have seen Jesus in the last two chapters in the great white throne of judgment and the marriage supper of the Lamb. He has appeared several times in the Book of Revelation pictured as a Lamb, pictured as a King, and pictured as a conqueror. He has been seen in many different ways. We learn many things about Jesus in this book. That is God's intention and the purpose for which the Revelation has been written. Anything else that we learn is just gravy. The second suggestion for understanding is to allow Revelation to interpret itself. My third suggestion is that as you study concepts that are in this book, don't consider them as foreign to the rest of the Bible. For instance, many things in the Bible are not literal. As an example, one of my favorite verses from the Psalms says,

> *"My Lord owns all of the cattle on a thousand hills."*

None of us would take that to literally limit God to only a thousand hills or that the ownership was literal and God was just a rancher. That is not the point of the lesson of the Psalm. The point is that there is a vastness to God's creation and he owns all of it. Understanding that should help to understand that the 1000 years is not literal either. Thus the other scriptures should help us understand the things that are in the Book of Revelation.

In Chapter 21, John says,

> *"Now I saw a new heaven and a new earth."*

Chapters 21 and 22 tell us about a beautiful place called heaven. However, the picture of heaven is presented in figurative terms such that a physical being can appreciate a spiritual place. He continues,

> *"For the first heaven and the first earth had passed away."*

There is not going to be an earth and heaven after the judgment. There will be a new heaven and a new earth. Also, there was no more sea. There are three references in the Book of Revelation to the sea. In Revelation chapter 4 in the throne room of God, we read about the throne with the rainbow behind it and the elders down either side and there was in front of the throne a sea like crystal. It was an undisturbed sea and totally calm. The second time we see the sea is in Revelation 15:2. And the sea is troubled. It had fire on it and in it are the saints that are being resurrected and the trial by fire of our works is being shown. Then, in Revelation 21, there is no more sea. We get a view of the new heaven and the sea is gone. Why is it gone? It is because death and Hades were cast into the hell fire. There is no need for the gulf that separated the wicked and the good in Hades. No need for the passage that our spirit has to make through the test of fire after our death.

I have always enjoyed watching the television series Star Trek. On the program was an engineer for the spacecraft named Scotty. When the space explorers would visit a planet and were ready to return to the spacecraft in orbit, they would click their communicator and say, "Beam me up Scotty." All of the sudden they would appear spaceship. That is the sea folks. Beam me up Scotty. Similar to that show, I imagine at death, we pass through the sea and end up in Hades either in Abraham's bosom or in torment. Beam me up Jesus. So now that death is gone, there is no need for the sea any longer. There is no more physical. Everything is spiritual.

Then, I John saw the Holy City, the New Jerusalem coming down out of heaven from God prepared as a bride adorned for her husband. Who is the bride of Christ? It is the church. Then what is the New Jerusalem? The New Jerusalem is dwelling place of the church. It is the city of the kingdom of Christ. It is a spiritual place for all the physical things have passed away. These physical descriptions that we read of New Jerusalem are intended to help us understand what this spiritual place is like. I heard a loud voice from heaven saying,

> *"Behold, the tabernacle of God is with men, and He will dwell with them, and they shall be His people."*

God will be there and dwell with us. He will be our God and wipe away every tear from our eyes. There shall be no more death. No sorrow. No dying. There shall be no more pain for the former things have passed away. When we consider heaven, we think of a place of joy and happiness. We think of a place with no pain or suffering. We think about a paradise, and about how wonderful it will be.

In verse 5, He who sat on the throne said,

> *"Behold, I make all things new."*

I don't want this old tabernacle or tent that I am wearing to house my spirit on earth. I don't want it back. I don't want it restored or put back like it was. I want a new body, for my new creature in Christ. My physical body while living on earth is God's tabernacle or temple where His Spirit dwells in me (1 Corinthians 3 and 6). Paul called the indwelling of God's Spirit my down payment. When you receive a down payment or earnest it means that more is coming. The more is that I will dwell in New Jerusalem in the presence of all the Godhead. God will be the light and we will dwell in His tabernacle.   There are several scriptural references in the Old Testament prophecies that are being fulfilled in these verses. Remember that Jesus is the Spirit of prophecy.

He who sat on the throne said to me,

126

"And He said to me, 'Write, for these words are true and faithful.' And He said to me, 'It is done!'"

This is the end of the story again. Jesus is the alpha and the omega, the beginning and the end. Jesus will give of the fountain of the water of life freely to him who thirsts. In John 4, Jesus told the Samaritan woman that He would give her living water and she would thirst no more. Not literal water, but knowledge and understanding. I don't think a spiritual being needs physical water, but he does thirst for knowledge of God. The cowardly, the unbelieving, the abominable, the murderers, the sexually immoral, the sorcerers, the idolaters and all liars shall have their part in the lake, which burns with fire and brimstone, which is the second death. This is a repeat of the words about a second death. I do not want to go there and I do not want you to go there. It is not an accommodating place.

"Then one of the seven angels who had the seven bowls filled with the seven last plagues came to me and talked with me, saying, 'Come, I will show you the bride, the Lamb's wife.' And he carried me away in the Spirit to a great and high mountain, and showed me the great city, the holy Jerusalem, descending out of heaven from God, having the glory of God. Her light was like a most precious stone, like a jasper stone, clear as crystal. Also she had a great and high wall with twelve gates, and twelve angels at the gates, and names written on them, which are the names of the twelve tribes of the children of Israel: three gates on the east, three gates on the north, three gates on the south, and three gates on the west."

That is very similar to the arrangement of the tabernacle in the Old Testament. Three of the tribes camped on each of the four cardinal sides of the tabernacle. There weren't any gates then because the people could not go in and out. Only priests could go in. But in New Jerusalem the four walls have been opened and gates installed. The gates are open all day and there is no night there. There is now no need to limit the relationship of God and His people. There is no more need for a mediator. The mediators in the Old Testament were priests. The mediator in the New Testament is Christ. However, in the church we all are a royal priesthood. In New Jerusalem we will have constant access to God.

The wall of the city had twelve foundations and on them were the names of twelve apostles of the Lamb. We have gates with the names of the twelve tribes and foundations with the names of the twelve apostles. These went together to produce God's plan. The foundations were of precious stones reminiscent of the twelve jewels on the breastplate of the High Priest in Exodus 28:17-20. He who talked with me had a gold reed to measure the city, its gates and its walls. The city is laid out in a square. Its length is as great as its breadth. He measured the city with a reed twelve thousand furlongs. Its length, breadth and height are equal. Twelve thousand furlongs is about 1,500 miles on the side. That is a big city. If you calculated how many people have lived since the beginning of time, and all of them were given a portion of the city, each one of them would possess more than a cubic mile. Can you imagine owning a cubic mile with a mansion made by God? That is what God has in store for the faithful whose names are in the Lamb's Book of Life.

> *"Let not your heart be troubled; you believe in God, believe also in Me. In My Father's house are many mansions; if it were not so, I would have told you. I go to prepare a place for you. And if I go and prepare a place for you, I will come again and receive you to Myself; that where I am, there you may be also." (John 14)*

The wall of the city measured 144 cubits as measured by the angel. The wall was also gold and jasper and precious stones. Inside the city, the streets were gold and the city was of pure gold and the saved walked in it. This gilded description is John's attempt to express in physical terms what He saw in this spiritual city prepared for God and His saints. Don't you want to go there?

John has been describing how God cares for the saved in eternity. First He describes the perfect fellowship we have with God. We dwell together in the same city. He is our light and there is no darkness there. He then describes the relationship that we have with God there. There are no tears. There is no dying. There is no sorrow. God is dwelling with us and it is a place of good fellowship. We also have perfect protection. Heaven is a place where there is no fear. There is no concern for the things that might destroy us. The great walls and angel guards insure that nothing that defiles can enter. There is also perfect provision. In the world of today, provision varies from person to person. We have wealthy people, middle class people poor people. They are mixed together in our society, but with God the provision is perfect.

In Chapter 22, John continues,

> *"And he showed me a pure river of water of life, clear as crystal, proceeding from the throne of God and of the Lamb. In the middle of its street, and on either side of the river, was the tree of life, which bore twelve fruits, each tree yielding its fruit every month. The leaves of the tree were for the healing of the nations. And there shall be no more curse, but the throne of God and of the Lamb shall be in it, and His servants shall serve Him. They shall see His face, and His name shall be on their foreheads. There shall be no night there: They need no lamp nor light of the sun, for the Lord God gives them light. And they shall reign forever and ever."*

This is the conclusion of the description of heaven begun in Chapter 21. Heaven is a great walled city 1,500 miles foursquare where all of the saints live. It is the place where God dwells, where there is no sin, no sickness and no sorrow. There is spiritual food that heals and maintains eternal life. It contains the tree of life that was removed from the Garden of Eden and we can partake of it and never die. John describes trees which are planted along the road beside the river that flows from the throne. It is a most beautiful scene.

There is a highway there and on each side of the highway there are trees planted. In the fall, I enjoy driving down the road in front of my house when the trees which overhang the road begin to change to that brilliant orange. It is absolutely gorgeous for a week or so as those trees change colors and reflect the fall sunlight. It makes me imagine what Heaven must be like. These trees that are planted alongside the golden road bear in all of seasons of the year. Every month there are twelve manners of fruit. Twelve seems to be a magical number in Revelation. It is the number of God and man to remind us of our relationship to the one who made us. In heaven, just like on earth, there will be different nations and groups of people. We talked earlier about the rewards in heaven; how we grow to be more appreciative of some things than others. Perhaps these nations respect our abilities to praise and enjoy and feel comfortable with our surroundings. Now to prevent disputes and wars the leaves of the trees provide healing. Heaven is a place of joy, peace, and happiness, a place where there is no struggle and strife.

REVELATION – CHAPTER 22

So we come to the end of the Book of Revelation. The first five verses of chapter 22 go with chapter 21 so we included them there. The epilogue begins in verse six. John converses with both the angel messenger and Jesus. At the start of the dialogue, the comment is made that God sent his angel to show unto his servants the things which must shortly be done. This comment on the surface may seem to validate the historical interpretative approach where the prophecies are taken to be the events surrounding the destruction of Jerusalem and the fall of Rome. We haven't followed that timeline. We rather have proposed a timeline that takes us throughout history. Consider that the Bible speaks of our life as a vapor, as a weaver's shuttle. Consider that Peter says that with the Lord a day is as a thousand years and a thousand years as a day. Consider that a man's days are three score and ten and if by matter of strength it might be four score. An eternal being does not consider time the same way that we do. Is a short time an hour, a day, a year, 100 years or 1,000 years? As one who turned 65 this last year, I can testify that after birth the 65th birthday comes shortly. In addition, what are the "these things" which the angel says comes shortly. If it is New Jerusalem that was just discussed, then it hasn't happened yet. Or if it is the casting of Satan into Hell, that hasn't happened yet. Even the historical approach does not satisfy the literal interpretation of the words. So, I believe the angel speaking from God's perspective of time.

Three times in this chapter, Jesus says that He comes quickly. Many look at this and assume a near term or quick coming. The word "quickly" is an adverb which describes how a verb operates. When Jesus does come, there will be no time to prepare. He will come as a thief. When His coming begins, it will happen quickly. These adverbs say nothing as to when but rather as to how He will come. In Revelation 11:14, the third woe comes quickly after the second. When it comes, there will be no delay, no waiting period. Jesus warns us to be prepared for He will come quickly.

John is spoken to by both the angel and Jesus. In verse 12,

> *"And behold, I am coming quickly."*

The I, refers to Jesus and in verse 16 he says,

> *"I, Jesus."*

Often in the visions, John is called by a voice from heaven. The voice which came out of heaven we see again at the end of the book and it is Jesus. John's revelations begin and end with Jesus. Jesus is the spirit of the prophecy. The angel, who speaks to John here, is described in verse 9 of the previous chapter as one of the seven angels, which had the seven bowls filled with the seven last plaques and he talked with me saying come hither and I will show you. It is the angel who has been showing. There was a voice from heaven prior to the angel who introduced the vision and then the angel comes and shows John the things of the holy city that comes down out of heaven.

When John attempts to bow down and worship the angel, the angel stops him and says, "See that you do not do that, for I am your fellow servant. This is not the first time this has happened to John. This is the second time in the Book of Revelation where John has attempted to worship an angel. As soon as the angel refuses, Jesus speaks to John again. Jesus describes Himself as the Alpha and the Omega. This is not the first time Jesus calls himself the Alpha and the Omega. Jesus is the beginning and the end. Being the alpha and omega is related to the numerology we have discussed earlier. We think numbers are for counting, but the Jews and Greeks considered numbers as concepts. Alpha and omega are the beginning and end of the alphabet. They represented the smallest number and the largest number. Jesus' words mean that He is eternal, that He will always be here. Jesus is an eternal being. He was at the beginning and He will be at the end.

Jesus offers an invitation or a curse to us. He says,

> "And the Spirit and the bride say, 'Come!' And let him who hears say, 'Come!' And let him who thirsts come. Whoever desires let him take the water of life freely."

Notice how the invitation is offered. There are no scriptures that command an invitation for our assembly. There are examples of invitations. In Acts chapter 2 Peter preached on the day of Pentecost. As the church assembled, there was preaching. Then how was the invitation extended? The assembly said,

> "Men and brethren, what shall we do?"

The assembly asked the apostles. In the invitation in this chapter, those who are thirsty were asked to come. We discover that the invitation often comes not as some formal thing, but something totally different. The thirsty call you on the phone. They approach you before or after the service. A couple of weeks ago I received a telephone call with a request from the nursing home to administer a baptism for an older resident of the home.

We also find the bride and the spirit saying come. Yes, the church is saying come. The invitation goes out through the church and through the Spirit. The word, the gospel of Jesus is offering the invitation. Peter preached the word, the gospel of Jesus and those who heard, those who were thirsty came. Whosoever will let him come.

Jesus then says,

> "If anyone adds to these things, God will add to him the plagues that are written in this book; and if anyone takes away from the words of the book of this prophecy, God shall take away his part from the Book of Life, from the holy city, and from the things which are written in this book."

Some say this curse just applies to the Book of Revelation. Others say it applies to the whole Bible. It certainly applies to the prophecies of the book of Revelation, but in principle it applies to the whole Bible. When John wrote the words of Jesus, Jesus was talking about that prophecy that John had just received. No doubt about that. However, the principle is that we are not to tamper with God's word. Alexander Campbell is attributed as saying, "We speak where the Bible speaks and we are silent when the Bible is silent." It is easy to speak where the Bible speaks, but much harder to be silent when the Bible is silent. We all sometimes quote from the book of opinions.

He that testifies says,

> *"Surely I am coming quickly."*

We need to be prepared at all times. Even so, come, Lord Jesus. Do we really desire the coming of Jesus? Will we be ready? The grace of our Lord Jesus Christ be with you all. Amen. "Hallelujah Anyway!"